PARENTING
ADULT CHILDREN

52-WEEK
DEVOTIONAL

Parenting ADULT CHILDREN

—

52-WEEK DEVOTIONAL

A Year of Devotions *for*
Navigating Your Changing Relationship

JAMIE CLOYD

ROCKRIDGE
PRESS

For general information on our other products and services or to obtain technical support, please contact our Customer Care Department within the United States at (866) 744-2665, or outside the United States at (510) 253-0500.

Rockridge Press publishes its books in a variety of electronic and print formats. Some content that appears in print may not be available in electronic books, and vice versa.

Interior and Cover Designer: John Calmeyer
Art Producer: Samantha Ulban
Editor: John Makowski
Production Editor: Ruth Sakata Corley
Production Manager: Lanore Coloprisco

All images used under license Shutterstock and iStock.
Author photo courtesy of Kayla Barker

Paperback ISBN: 978-1-63878-327-5
eBook ISBN: 978-1-63878-531-6
R0

I would
like to dedicate
this book to the
greatest parent of all,
our *Father God*.
I am honored
to be called
your son.

CONTENTS

INTRODUCTION

WELCOME TO YOUR 52-week devotional *Parenting Adult Children.* This helpful guide was written and structured as a tool to help parents of every kind of adult child, whether they have unexpectedly moved back home, have become emotionally distant, or need some special parental attention. Maybe things are solid and you want to keep it that way. All relationships grow and change; the connection to your child will continue to morph as they (and you!) mature. This Bible-centered devotional will help you navigate the issues and hurdles that can affect almost every parent-child relationship. If used regularly and consistently, you will develop healthy parenting and spiritual disciplines, such as studying scripture, using contemplation and prayer, and writing about your individual growth as a parent of adult children.

My name is Jamie Cloyd, and I am a 53-year-old parent of three adult children, along with my wife of 26 years. We have experienced most, if not all, of the struggles that parents go through, and with God's guiding hand, we feel we have produced a legacy of faith that will last for generations to come. The benefit of my personal experience is that I have placed and kept my faith in God the Father, the creator and sustainer of all life. I will walk with you for 52 weeks, sharing what I have learned from the Bible, as God's blueprint for marriage and family relationships are woven throughout the stories and messages in His Word. In my quest to know Him better, I have spent years studying and applying His truths to my life, and to my relationships with my children. I have been a youth pastor and teacher for much of my adult life. I lead a men's Bible study that has continued to grow for six years now. I am also a Certified Christian Life Coach with a focus on helping men discover the keys to a happy and successful life through placing faith in God and applying His Word.

This 52-week devotional is tailored to Christian parents seeking wisdom, guidance, and inspiration from the Bible. It is laid out in a format that will lead you through the scriptures, challenge you to place your faith in the principles found in them, and encourage you to take responsibility for your relationships through weekly action plans. The devotional addresses several hard issues that parents of adult children face, with topics such as: anxiety, depression, healthy boundaries, having difficult conversations, and finding peace, just to name a few. It will assist you and challenge you to search out what God has to say to us in His Word: the Holy Bible. By actively participating in each devotion, you will spend time with God in reading the Bible and in prayer, taking actions that will positively improve your relationship with God and with your adult child.

How is the Bible the authority on parenting adult children, you might ask? You will see in this devotional that "All Scripture is God-breathed and is useful for teaching, rebuking, correcting and training in righteousness, so that the servant of God may be thoroughly equipped for every good work" (2 Timothy 3:16–17). You will also discover that "the word of God is alive and active. Sharper than any double-edged sword, it penetrates even to dividing soul and spirit, joints and marrow; it judges the thoughts and attitudes of the heart" (Hebrews 4:12).

We have been blessed with many good translations of the Bible. Some are literal translations while others are paraphrased to shed light on the truths found in today's terminology. This devotional will quote primarily from the New International Version, but feel free to follow along with your favorite translation as we journey through the scriptures together.

HOW TO USE
THIS BOOK

TO GET THE most benefit from this book, I recommend you set aside some quiet time, without distractions, and move at your own pace. Begin with a prayer for God to open the eyes of your understanding during each devotion.

I encourage you not to rush through. Take time to reflect on the message in each section, as you are lead through a Bible verse, commentary, reflections, an action of the week, and a guided prayer. As you move through each week, listen for what God is saying to you in each step. He will speak directly to you! Take time to listen for His voice in your heart/spirit, and then respond. Above all, as you devote yourself to spending time with God and the Bible, you may have to stop in the middle of a devotion for whatever reason. Don't get discouraged if you don't complete the week's devotion. Make any necessary schedule changes, and get back into it. You might also struggle at times during these devotions with feelings of guilt or agitation as you learn to undo a negative self-image and learn how to become a better parent and child of God yourself. Be patient with yourself, and forgive yourself. Make a commitment to yourself and your adult children to still go back and complete each section of that week's devotion. I encourage you to use a journal as you work through this devotional to record all of your thoughts in one place.

It's designed to start any time of the year; no need to wait until January 1. Dive in!

LET GOD
GUIDE YOU

AS YOU BEGIN your one-year journey through this devotional, you have a promise from God that He will lead you. The Lord says, "I will instruct you and teach you in the way you should go; I will counsel you with my loving eye on you" (Psalm 32:8). You belong to the Lord Jesus Christ, and you have the ability to hear his voice and follow Him. There will be times a Bible verse or section will stand out to you. When that happens, ask, "Lord, what are you showing me? What are you saying to me right now?" Then listen quietly for a moment as He leads you into deeper revelation and relationship with Him when you follow what He says.

It is my prayer for you, the reader, that this devotional will draw you closer to God, that your faith will grow stronger, and that it will encourage you to never give up. God answers prayer!

the
DEVOTIONS

When Grown Children Come Home

Fathers, do not exasperate your children; instead, bring them up in the training and instruction of the Lord.

— Ephesians 6:4

COMMENTARY

As one who once was an adult child who returned home, I can testify to the truth of this verse. After my divorce at the age of 22, I had to humble myself and ask my parents if I could move back home. When kids move back home, the grown child likely already has a cloud of failure looming over them. The last thing they need is to hear "I told you so" from mom or dad. What they need in that moment is tenderness and love. As parents, you already love them deeply, right? Show them by accepting them back without the arm-long list of your house rules. Your parenting tactics need to change because the old dynamics have changed. Try reaffirming their dignity at the start, to establish mutual trust.

Sometimes younger adult children need to come back home for other reasons, such as colleges closing campuses unexpectedly, or maybe they need to regroup and sort out their future plans. You should feel honored if they want to come back home! It is a testament to good parenting when they choose to come home to you, instead of going elsewhere. It means they feel safe and, ideally, wanted. Lovingly offer them time and space to exercise their newly found freedom.

Have you done your best to raise your children by biblical standards? Let me clarify: "biblical standards" does not mean a strict set of rules with harsh punishments for failures; it means always extending unconditional love and grace to your kids. That is, after all, how God loves us! Romans 5:8 says, "But God demonstrates his own love for us in this: While we were still sinners, Christ died for us." Your unconditional love is key to surviving, if not embracing, your new living situation.

Regardless of the reason they want or need to come back home, use this opportunity to reassure them of your love and support. Do your best to approach conversations with a positive spin, speaking adult to adult, remembering they aren't little kids anymore.

REFLECTIONS

✢ Whether your grown children have come home or not, in what ways are they showing you that they still need you as their parent? How does that make you feel?

✢ How, by your own example, can you show your grown children the attributes of their Heavenly Father?

ACTION OF THE WEEK

Make it a priority this week to show your grown children that you love them deeply. This could be an action, such as washing and servicing their car, or an intangible, such as a deep conversation with them about their thoughts, plans, and dreams where you spend concentrated time listening, without adding your input or opinions.

GUIDED PRAYER

Father God, help me understand Your love for me so that I can reflect Your perfect love to my children. Give me wisdom to know how to best help them along their own path, and help remind me, as in Psalm 127:3, that my children are a gift and a reward from You.

The Prodigal Son

So he returned home to his father. And while he was still a long way off, his father saw him coming. Filled with love and compassion, he ran to his son, embraced him, and kissed him.

— *Luke 15:20 (NLT)*

COMMENTARY

The story of the prodigal son in Luke 15 tells the story of a young man who got his inheritance before his father died. The son wasted all his money on wild living, off in a distant country. Verse 14 says, "About the time his money ran out, a great famine swept over the land, and he began to starve." He took a job feeding pigs and became so hungry, he would have eaten the pigs' food. Verse 16 says "no one gave him anything." This is a story of hitting rock bottom.

It is hard to watch your adult child hit their own rock bottom. I know because I had to allow my own son to do just that as he battled alcoholism. It was a painful, heart-wrenching time for me and my wife. There are a couple of insights I gleaned from this story that may help you. First was the realization that you can't keep catching them when they fall. Eventually, you have to allow them to experience the entire process for themselves. Catching them before they hit bottom only prolongs the process to recovery. Second, I learned that the father in the story did not go chasing after his son. The only thing any father can do in this situation is pray for their child's protection while they are gone, and pray and believe they will return again. I had to do this for two years when my son moved across the country and would not speak to me. I can tell you that it wasn't easy to keep the faith after two years with no answers to prayer, but I can tell you that prayer works—eventually

4

he did return home! I met him at the door with a huge hug, and our relationship has been fully restored!

If you are living out this story as I did, don't get discouraged. Most people think prayer is their last hope—but it should be the starting point. I can say for a fact that prayer is the most powerful thing you can do when facing these circumstances. Pray daily over your son or daughter, in faith, believing and expecting them to return again. Don't give up!

REFLECTIONS

✢ If they are facing turmoil right now, do you think your son or daughter has hit their bottom? Do you think you'll be able to watch from afar as/when they do?

✢ Are you covering him or her in prayer? It can be hard to see past the pain they are inflicting on themselves and others (including you perhaps), but they need your prayers now more than ever.

ACTION OF THE WEEK

Write down your deepest feelings about your adult son or daughter who might be going through tough times. Pray about what you wrote, lifting it to God. You might even write out the prayer and keep it in your Bible.

GUIDED PRAYER

Lord give me wisdom to know how to best help _____ during this hard time. Help me learn to pray effectively for _____ and give me strength to keep praying. Amen.

When the Last Chick Leaves the Nest

Whoever fears the LORD has a secure fortress,
and for their children it will be a refuge.
— *Proverbs 14:26*

COMMENTARY

After our youngest daughter, Julia, left for college, my wife went through a period of sadness. It's called "empty nest syndrome." I was there to cheer her up and reassure her that we were going to be okay, that this is just a part of life all parents have to go through. After a few months went by, my wife was feeling better, but she and my friends started asking me, "What's wrong?" They knew I wasn't myself. But I didn't know what it was from or about, really, so I would tell them it was nothing. My wife saw it, my close friends saw it, but I couldn't put my finger on it.

One day, sitting all alone at home, I started feeling deep sorrow, so I prayed and asked God what was wrong with me. I then understood that I deeply missed our daughter. She was, after all, my mini me! I felt that she didn't need me anymore, and as a dad, I was having an identity crisis. Did I do enough to prepare her for the world? Who would be her protector so far from home? Would we lose our special bond now that she's all grown up and moved on? Empty nest syndrome had finally caught up with me, too. I realized I had to deal with my sadness and loneliness; the syndrome can become deeply depressing if not handled properly.

Dealing with these emotions in a healthy way is key in discovering your new roles as parents of grown-up children. I chose to press into prayer and Bible study. I allowed myself to cry, and as awkward as it was, it actually felt good to release those feelings; it let me reset my thinking. Julia wrote me the sweetest card reassuring me that

I will always be her daddy, and that she takes comfort in knowing that I will always be there for her no matter what. That sweet card, written from her heart to mine, gave me extra confidence to face the next chapter of life! I can't help but think her letter was yet another answered prayer.

The feelings of loneliness and sadness are very real when it comes to the empty nest. Sure, you can fill your time with activities to keep your mind busy and preoccupied. But eventually, when all is quiet and it's time for bed, and you are left with your thoughts and feelings, you will have to process those suppressed emotions. Can you do that in a way that will allow for your growth?

REFLECTIONS

* Have you experienced a form of empty nest syndrome? How? Were you expecting to?

* If you've been dealing with it, how are you processing the emotions of loss, sadness, and loneliness in a healthy way? Are there people or resources you may need to turn to for help?

ACTION OF THE WEEK

If you have or are experiencing empty nest syndrome, write down the steps you can or are taking to navigate through this process in a healthy way. If you have not yet experienced it, you are bound to, so write out a plan of action to prepare for it when it comes. If you lack wisdom, ask God (James 1:5)!

GUIDED PRAYER

Father God, help me understand my new role as a parent of grown children who have moved away. Help me process my feelings so I can emotionally support my independent child in a positive way and avoid depression. Thank You, Father, amen.

Quality Time

For the Father loves the Son and shows him all he does.
Yes, and he will show him even greater works than
these, so that you will be amazed.

— *John 5:20*

COMMENTARY

As a family, we've always enjoyed vacation trips with our children. Though we enjoyed every trip, there were times when it was hard to please everyone. Even after all our children have grown up and moved out, we still cherish getting to take family trips with our ever-expanding family!

It was on one of these new family trips that I got to enjoy some quality time with my son, Josh. We were all staying in a cabin in Ruidoso, New Mexico: my wife, our two daughters, our son-in-law, our son, and our first grandbaby. One day I took my son fishing at Lake Alta to catch some lake trout. We found a spot near the dam and I "set up camp." Josh moved down the shoreline about thirty yards and started fishing. We were in shallow water near the bank, and neither of us was having any luck.

I set up what is called a sinker rig and cast my bait out to a dark patch a little farther offshore. This dark patch was a grassy ditch where I started landing trout almost as soon as my bait hit the target. Josh came over to where I was, and I showed him how to set up a sinker rig. We went back to his spot, and I showed him where to cast. He got his first bite almost instantaneously! That changed everything and sparked an excitement in him I hadn't seen in some time. He would catch one and release it, then I would catch one and release it. We did this back-and-forth competition and got loud as we would yell to the other, "Fish on!" At one point, I threw out a double line and caught two trout at the same time. We caught about fourteen fish in all and had such a great time fishing together.

Quality time like this allows your parent-child relationship to blossom, even as they grow up and the dynamics of the relationship change. Making it a point to create shared experiences—even if it's just teaching how to set up a sinker rig—is an almost foolproof method for sustaining those relationships.

REFLECTIONS

- ✦ When was the last time you spent real quality time with your children independently? Was it planned or spontaneous? Who initiated it?

- ✦ How can you go about making future "together time" plans with them?

ACTION OF THE WEEK

Write down realistic plans and ideas for creating quality time adventures with each of your grown children—even if it's in your own backyard. Quality time doesn't need to cost a dime; it doesn't have to take too much calendar time either (it's not like I'm suggesting a private 10-day getaway). Your child simply needs to know you're making special time just for them, and only them.

GUIDED PRAYER

Father, You are the best father! I want to have more quality time adventures with you. Help remind me You are always there for me. Will You plan something for us—You and me—to enjoy together as we make new memories together? Amen.

How to Have Difficult Conversations

A gentle answer turns away wrath,
but a harsh word stirs up anger.
— *Proverbs 15:1*

COMMENTARY

No one likes to have hard conversations with those we love. It can be a lot like juggling knives—if not handled properly, someone is bound to get hurt. We tend to avoid the difficult conversations because we feel we can't achieve the desired outcome, or we fear the repercussions may be like striking a hornet's nest.

I was recently asked to mediate such a conversation between two of my friends. I am not saying I am adequately equipped to manage hard conversations myself (just ask my wife). But I gave them a couple of analogies that are useful in any conversation, both dealing with taking control and steering the conversation, and setting or managing the "temperature" of it. Consider using these steps when facing a difficult topic with any of your children:

1. Imagine you want to go for a hike in the mountains with your child and need to drive there. If you are the one driving and want to control the direction you are heading, you have to take the steering wheel and guide the car. If your child keeps grabbing at the wheel, you are likely to crash. But if you want to be the one driving, you have to take the keys, get in the driver's seat, start the car, and invite the other to go with you. If it is not working out, you can simply pull the car over until you can safely reach the destination. It's the same with a tough conversation. You can practice steering the conversation by asking direct, closed-ended questions that require the other to thoughtfully formulate a response. Then, by asking open-ended questions, you allow the child to offer detailed directions on how to get there or where to go next.

2. Now envision the climate control in your car as a way to control the temperature of the conversation. If the conversation starts getting too heated, you can control the thermostat by being the one who cools down the situation—by applying this week's Bible verse. If you allow things to get too hot using harsh words, one or both of you will say things you might regret; pausing, taking a breath, and choosing gentle and kind words will cool it down.

Juggling knives requires lots of practice in a safe space. So does driving in mountainous terrain. Practice having hard conversations with a good friend first, so you will be better equipped when the occasion arises in your own family dynamic.

REFLECTIONS

✦ Think back to the last hard conversation you had with your child. How well did you do in steering it and controlling the thermostat? Could you try the same or a similar conversation again, using new "driving" techniques?

✦ We all have to have difficult conversations sometimes. How can you put Proverbs 15:1 into practice?

ACTION OF THE WEEK

Ask a good friend to help you practice these techniques by simulating a difficult conversation you may need to have with one of your children.

GUIDED PRAYER

Father God, help me learn how to control my temper, and my choice of words, the next time I have to have a difficult conversation. Amen.

Mirror Reflections

*For now we see only a reflection in a mirror; then
we shall see face to face. Now I know in part;
then I shall know fully, even as I am fully known.*

— *1 Corinthians 13:12*

COMMENTARY

All too often we grow up with the idea that when we have our own children, we will parent differently than our parents did with us, only to realize that we look a lot like mom or dad after all. We said things like "I will never scream, *'I said be quiet!'*" but as adults we hear those very words escape our lips!

We might have been blessed to have Godly parents who did a great job raising us, or we might have had the worst parents imaginable. Whatever that looks like for you, you have a choice to do things differently, to be the type of parents you needed growing up. Even now, your parenting doesn't have to mirror the parenting you received; it can and should reflect a healthy relationship with God. He is, after all, the best parent ever! His Word offers wisdom and training in all areas of life, so that no matter what your childhood looked like, your parenting can reflect a genuine, healthy, loving relationship with Him.

No matter how hard we try or study up, our parenting skill set is imperfect. We will always have areas that need improvement. Moving past our failures and fears as parents and striving to be ever better should be the ongoing goal, trusting God to make up for our weaknesses.

When I was young, my parents had the best intentions but were very naive and didn't know many of the things I was getting involved in, like parties, drugs, drinking, and smoking, all at a very young age. As an adult parent, I was always on the lookout for signs of that in my own children. I expected to see my own reflection in them. Thanks be to God I did not! I saw how God can redeem broken, damaged goods and help me raise three awesome children who reflect our father God instead.

The more time we spend with God, in his Word, in His presence, in His glory, the more we will start to reflect His image to others! In 2 Corinthians 3:18 it says, "And we all, who with unveiled faces contemplate the Lord's glory, are being transformed into his image with ever-increasing glory, which comes from the Lord, who is the Spirit."

REFLECTIONS

✛ How much does your parenting reflect your own parents? How do you feel about that? Is it time to break the chain of unhealthy connections, or are you proud their legacy lives on?

✛ How much of your parenting reflects the image of God? Is there room for improvement?

ACTION OF THE WEEK

Set a goal and make it a priority to spend _____ (set amount of time) each day reading the Bible and meditating throughout the day on what you read. At the end of the day, write down any insights or wisdom you learned that day.

GUIDED PRAYER

Father God, please polish Your reflection in me so others can see Your glory and goodness in me. Lord make me more and more like you. Amen.

Knock, Knock!

Here I am! I stand at the door and knock.
If anyone hears my voice and opens the door, I will
come in and eat with that person, and they with me.
— *Revelation 3:20*

COMMENTARY

One morning I woke myself and my wife up by laughing out loud in my sleep. She asked me what was so funny, and I said, "Jesus told me a joke!" As I recalled the dream, I said, "He asked me if I knew why he stands at the door and knocks." To Jesus I said, "No, why?" And he replied, "Because I have given you the keys to the Kingdom!" I could still hear him laughing at his own joke as I awoke to my own laughter. Although you might think it strange, that really happened!

The Lord is so mighty and powerful, but He is also a perfect gentleman. He desires a deep relationship with us, but He respects our choice of free will so much that He will only knock on the door of our hearts, hoping that we will invite Him in. He could kick down our doors announcing His redemption (His purchase of our souls) and demand our worship. He doesn't force Himself on us, however; He patiently waits for our invitation to have a relationship with Him! As we spend time in prayer, we get to know His heart and mind. It is, and should be, the most important relationship we ever have in this life and the one to come, because all our other relationships can and will be affected by this relationship. If we develop a connection with Him, we can learn to share healthy relationships, with our children and with friends.

As parents, we should try to be more like Jesus and patiently knock on the doors of our children's hearts, desiring for them to let us inside to enjoy a real relationship with them. We know that demanding they let us in won't work; it will just push our children further away. When our children see us spending time in our own relationship with the Lord, it becomes a model for our children, allowing them to see how to develop their own healthy relationship with the Father.

Whether or not your relationship is such that Jesus tells you jokes in your sleep, the fact is, He loves each of us uniquely, and He longs for His relationship with each of us to go deeper and deeper as we spend time with Him.

REFLECTIONS

✢ Have you heard the knock on your heart's door and invited Jesus in?

✢ If not, He remains patiently knocking. Will you open the door to the greatest relationship of all?

ACTION OF THE WEEK

Find new ways to knock on the door of your children's hearts and, if accepted, make the time you spend together special for both of you. Maybe that looks like inviting them to go have a coffee or an ice cream and just hang out for a while.

GUIDED PRAYER

Lord Jesus, help me hear and answer Your knock on my door. I want to develop a deeper relationship with You, so I invite You to come into my heart and spend time with me. Amen.

When Despair Takes Hold

Turn to me and be gracious to me,
for I am lonely and afflicted.
— *Psalm 25:16*

COMMENTARY

When parents really love their children, they will do just about anything to help them.

Our oldest was off attending a music recording school in Phoenix, Arizona. When I got the call, "Dad, I want to come home," I tried to talk him into toughing it out just a few more months. I mentioned all the money that would be wasted. I tried a pep talk. But when he said, "Dad, I'm having suicidal thoughts," I said I would be there the next morning on the first flight in. I immediately booked my ticket. The next morning, we loaded as much of his belongings as we could cram into his little Kia Rio and headed back home.

I had known those same feelings myself as a young man, and I knew that bringing him home was the only option we had. We are never promised an easy way in this life, but when our children fall on hard times, we step up and do whatever we can to help them. Sometimes that means bringing them back home, while other times it might be checking them into rehab. It is hard to see your children hurting and you want to do something.

If I had not known how he really felt, I could have gotten mad and told him to suck it up and deal with it. Many parents in this situation might react just this way, and the outcome could be tragic. Being able to silence your personal opinions and listen objectively and empathetically to your child's heart is the first step in getting them the help they need. I do not wish for all parents to know suicidal thoughts as I do. However, I do encourage all parents to learn to detect the early warning signs, and know how to be prepared to help them if the need ever arises. It is not morbid to reflect on your child's suicidal thoughts in order to better understand how to really help them—and possibly prevent that very thing. Learning to catch early warning signs of suicide might allow you to help or intervene before it's too late.

If you ever suspect, or have intuitive feelings as a parent, that your child is considering suicide, seek help now while there is time. Use every tool at your disposal to equip yourself to be able to help when it really counts. The National Suicide Prevention Hotline is available 24 hours a day, in Spanish and English: 1-800-273-8255. A great website with links, resources, and information can be found in this book's Resources section (page 107).

REFLECTIONS

- Everyone is susceptible to depression. It's not anything to be ashamed of or hide. Have you ever spoken openly with your children about depression and suicide?

- If not, will you learn about the topic and make a plan to discuss it with your children this week?

ACTION OF THE WEEK

Make a plan to research and educate yourself on depression and suicide in teens and young adults. Libraries are a great resource, as are vetted online materials and videos.

GUIDED PRAYER

Father God, help me be equipped to understand depression and suicidal thoughts—if not for my own children, possibly for family or friends in need. Guide me in my studies. Amen.

Peace: The Great Equalizer

Peace I leave with you; my peace I give you.
I do not give to you as the world gives. Do not let
your hearts be troubled and do not be afraid.

— John 14:27

COMMENTARY

Parenting adult children can definitely be stressful. We can learn a valuable lesson from scuba divers.

Deep sea explorers must learn how to equalize the air pressure in their ears and lungs to avoid damage as they adjust to increasing pressure underwater. Equalization is crucial to avoid serious damage, like ruptured eardrums and lungs. The deeper the diver goes, the greater the pressure they experience, requiring that they continually equalize the pressure.

The same is true, spiritually speaking, when the pressures of life are pressing in on us from every angle, and our adult children are butting heads with us. We need the peace of God working on the inside to equalize the pressure and to avoid serious damage like depression, high blood pressure, anxiety, sickness, etc.

If we are lacking His peace, we will feel greater amounts of pressure and agitation from the world around us and will feel the pressure in our soul (mind, will, emotions). The peace of God has to be equal to or greater than the external pressures or we will receive temporary and even long-term damage.

Jesus said that we have the power to not let our hearts be troubled or afraid because His peace is the great equalizer! Imagine an old-fashioned scale that represents your heart. Stress or pressure is on one side, and God's peace on the other. The more the pressure increases, the greater the necessity for more of His peace to tip the scale in your favor.

With the added pressure of having your adult children needing attention or moving back home, it is crucial you learn to appropriate the peace of Christ in your heart. We read in John 14:27 that His peace is a gift. We just have to receive it! If you are not walking in His peace in this moment, pray and ask for a gift from God.

REFLECTIONS

✣ Do you know and walk in the peace that passes understanding?

✣ How will you spend time this week seeking greater peace in your heart and mind?

ACTION OF THE WEEK

Spend time this week praying over your grown child(ren), telling God what you need, and thanking Him for all He has done in their life. Experience God's peace, which exceeds anything we can understand. His peace will guard your hearts and minds as you live in Christ Jesus.

GUIDED PRAYER

My prayer for you: "May the God of hope fill you with all joy and peace as you trust in him, so that you may overflow with hope by the power of the Holy Spirit" (Romans 15:13). Amen.

Learning to Listen

My dear brothers and sisters, take note of this:
Everyone should be quick to listen, slow to speak
and slow to become angry.

— *James 1:19*

COMMENTARY

It is human nature to want to convince everyone else we are right. This is the source of many arguments, whether in marriage or in dealing with our children, coworkers, or friends. It is more important to us in the moment to want to convince the other person that we are right and they are wrong; they are usually doing the same thing to us.

To close our mouth and open our ears is a difficult discipline to learn at first. That is the context of this week's Bible verse. Oh, if we could learn this one truth and actually practice it! We could spare ourselves and those we love the harshness of arguments and fights. Even if you may be the one who is right under the circumstances, taking the opportunity to really listen to what the other has to say can possibly change the outcome. Usually, the other person is already defensive because they either presume to be right in their own mind or they expect an argument.

Learning to listen is hard enough, but the second part of that verse says we must be slow to speak. This is even harder to learn and practice. We tend to listen only to look for opportunities to interject our opinions, and we justify it by calling it dialog. I am so guilty of this one. When we are dealing with our adult children, this can be even harder to practice. They may well be in the wrong, but your pointing it out is only going to push them away. It might make them less likely to go to you for help in the future. Instead, try "biting your tongue" long enough for them to see reality for themselves. Eventually they will see that you were right and respect you more for not rubbing their nose in it.

The last part of this week's verse says we must be slow to anger. Man, it just gets harder and harder, right? Why does God expect so much from us?! I say that tongue-in-cheek. As believers, we are, or should be, growing in wisdom and grace. Try just starting with the first part, and practice listening. As we get better at maintaining self-control, we can take the rest of the verse step-by-step, until we get better at diffusing confrontations and actually having positive interactions with our family and children.

REFLECTIONS

✢ Hearing and listening are two different things. The words we hear can flow in one ear and out the other. Listening is taking those words and processing them with the goal of understanding them.

✢ Would your boss say that you are a good listener? Would your children?

ACTION OF THE WEEK

Write out James 1:19 on a sticky note and place it on your bathroom mirror or on the dash of your car, wherever it will be a constant reminder to put others first and seek to be a peacemaker.

GUIDED PRAYER

Father, empower me as I try to learn to be quick to listen, slow to speak, and slow to get angry. Amen.

When You Feel Forgotten by God

But when you pray, go into your room, close the door and pray to your Father, who is unseen. Then your Father, who sees what is done in secret, will reward you.

— Matthew 6:6

COMMENTARY

Walking by faith can be a time of lonely questioning. What I mean is, to walk by faith means not walking by sight. We have to rely on a God—who we cannot see—to be active in our circumstances, which is all we can see. It is normal, at times, to question God. It doesn't make you a bad Christian, and God won't smite you if you question Him!

King David questioned God many times in the Psalms, and God called him a man after his own heart. David said things like "O LORD, why do You stand so far away? Why do You hide when I am in trouble?" and "Why have You forgotten me? Why must I wander around in grief, oppressed by my enemies?" As Christians and parents, we are promised that our faith will be tested. We don't like to hear that, I know, but it is true. The book of James says that when our faith is tested, our endurance has a chance to grow. We are to let it grow, so that when our endurance is fully developed, we will be perfect and complete, lacking nothing.

During trying parenting times, it can be difficult to see the light at the end of the tunnel. It may look like everything is caving in on us and God has abandoned us in our hour of deepest need. This is when we need to double down and stay focused on our faith, by clinging to the promises of God! He is at work even if we can't see it.

There are many promises in the Bible, such as "I will not fail you or abandon you" and "the very hairs on your head are all numbered. So don't be afraid; you are more valuable to God than a whole flock of sparrows."

These are only two of many promises in the Word of God. There are many more you can search out in the scriptures. Read them and focus on them being fulfilled in His—not your—timing. When our faith is being tested, we must run to Him, not from Him, to see things change for the better. Our invisible God sees you in every situation and cares for you deeply.

REFLECTIONS

✢ Has your faith been tested recently? If so, write down how it was tested and how God answered.

✢ Can you think of a time you felt abandoned by God? Write it down and take it to Him in prayer. Ask Him to show you where He was at that time in your life.

ACTION OF THE WEEK

Write down at least five promises from the Bible that mean something special to you, and read them every day this week. (It's okay if you have to search for them online—just make sure it's from a credible source!) Try to memorize one or two.

GUIDED PRAYER

Father, increase my level of faith so I can believe and trust You more, especially when I feel like I've lost hope. Amen.

Our Words Are Powerful

*Gracious words are a honeycomb, sweet to
the soul and healing to the bones.*

— *Proverbs 16:24*

COMMENTARY

No matter their age, children seek the affirmation of their parents.
We all have that desire for approval and acceptance. As your children become adults, and they venture out into the world, their
experiences are new. They are interacting with the public on their
own, as adults now, and many of them become nervous and anxious.
It is unfamiliar territory and can be scary. Whether opening a checking account, signing their first lease on an apartment, or repainting a
room, each encounter holds a learning and growing opportunity. At
the same time, the potential for failure is also present. How can we
as parents help them navigate these grown-up adventures?

When my son was in his late teens and still at home, he asked
to borrow some tools to change the oil in his car for the first time.
I said sure and offered my assistance if needed. About twenty
minutes later, he walked into the house all aggravated with red, oily
hair. I may have chuckled for a second. I could have yelled at him to
not get that gooey mess on the floor, shamed him by saying "I knew
you'd need help," or had a myriad of unhelpful reactions. Instead,
I reassured him that he could do this. He wiped his hair as best he
could, and we went out to his car. I pointed out that there are two
drain plugs under there, one for motor oil and the other for trans-
mission fluid. I told him that he had learned that lesson already on
his own, and that it wasn't the end of the world. I assured him he
wouldn't make that mistake again! He has since changed his own oil
many times with confidence.

This simple example is just one of many experiences that turned into object lessons. It is easy to tear down another person to feel better about ourselves, even when it is our children. As parents we need to see the opportunity before us, to build up or to tear down, and make the right choice in the moment. Psalm 64:3 says, "They sharpen their tongues like swords and aim cruel words like deadly arrows." Our words can be used to harm or heal. We need to be mindful of this when we have learning and teaching opportunities with our children.

REFLECTIONS

I know some parents who would revel in such an experience, saying things like "I knew something like that would happen" and harshly laugh at their child without thinking. Those words would do damage. Instead of tearing them down, put yourself in their shoes for a minute. Think about what you would want to hear in that moment. If we season our words with grace, they will be sweet to the soul and edifying to the mind.

- When your own children have made a mess of something, have you chosen to speak words of blessing or cursing over them?
- Will you look for opportunities to bless them and speak pleasant words over them?

ACTION OF THE WEEK

Think of positive ways you can encourage your children this week. Maybe write them a note, text, or email about the good things you see in them. Tell them (in words!) you support them.

GUIDED PRAYER

Lord forgive me for speaking harmful words, and help me put a guard on my tongue. Amen.

Healthy Boundaries, Part 1

And the LORD God commanded the man, "You are free to eat from any tree in the garden; but you must not eat from the tree of the knowledge of good and evil, for when you eat from it you will certainly die."

— *Genesis 2:16–17*

COMMENTARY

In the beginning when God created the heavens and the earth, He created man in His image and likeness, and He had a close relationship with Adam and Eve. God is the best example of Biblical parenting. He loved them unconditionally, but He was also the first one to establish boundaries with his children. The Old Testament famously tells the story of God giving Moses the Ten Commandments on Mount Sinai. In fact, God gave his people many other rules to live by. These were known as statutes and laws and they were given to establish the boundaries set by a loving God to protect His people. Of course, it doesn't take long in reading the Bible to see that man is flawed by sinful choices.

As Christian parents, we do the same for our children if we love them and want to raise them to know and love God. We set boundaries when they are young, in hopes that by learning their choices have consequences, they will learn to make good or better choices in life.

As parents of adult children who live with us, the principle is the same, but the dynamics are different. We might set boundaries, such as "If you want to live in our house, you must pay rent." This is a common boundary parents use to teach financial responsibility. I remember my parents setting this very rule when I moved back in with them after my divorce at twenty-two years old. I did not like it, but it was a rule I had to abide by in order to stay with them. They took a set amount of my paycheck each month and put it into a savings account for me, because I would have cashed my check and spent it all on having fun. When I left home again, I had money set aside to help me get back on my feet. They used boundaries to teach me life lessons that I would have continued to struggle with down the road, if left to my own choices.

We all need to have healthy boundaries in our lives, not only to learn right from wrong but also that our choices have consequences. When our children become adults, they will need to understand why healthy boundaries must be respected, because as adults, their actions will have greater repercussions.

REFLECTIONS

+ If you were raised with certain boundaries set by your parents, what life lessons did you learn from them?

+ Have you and your partner set clearly defined boundaries with your adult children? Are the boundaries being respected? If not, what are the consequences?

ACTION OF THE WEEK

Write down the boundaries you have established for your children, along with the consequences for not respecting them. Take the time to clearly articulate them to your children; they may not even know those are your rules! Make sure they understand and agree to them.

GUIDED PRAYER

Lord, give me wisdom and resolve to set healthy boundaries with my adult children, and help me stick to them even when it gets difficult. Amen.

Healthy Boundaries, Part 2

*That is why a man leaves his father and mother and is
united to his wife, and they become one flesh.*
— Genesis 2:24

COMMENTARY

As Christian parents of adult children, we should do our best to
train up our children and direct them down the right path, teaching
them to love and respect the Lord. We stand on the promise that
when they are old, they won't depart from it. Then they grow up and
hopefully get married and begin their own lives and families.

Many times, it is hard as parents not to want to keep on
instructing them in the way they should go. After all, we hopefully did a good job raising them, so why not keep at it? It's
natural to want to help them learn how to be parents. Sometimes
we subconsciously insert ourselves too far into their lives, and
resentment and frustration develop in our children. But grand-
parenting is not a chance to correct your own flaws as a parent in
the lives of your grandchildren.

I remember having this conversation with my parents when I
was a single dad living with them after my divorce. I tried my best
to explain to them that I did respect and welcome their opinions,
but in the end, I may not do things the way they want me to. I would
make my own decisions and deal with the consequences as an adult.
They did have lots of great advice after all, but I felt the tension
between heeding their advice and making my own decisions as
a parent.

For example: You might have allowed dessert before dinner for
your children, but your children may decide no dessert at all. We
might strongly disagree with their choices on raising their children,

but if we want our children to continue to spend time with us and share their new family with us, we need to learn to respect their boundaries as parents.

It's not like babies come with an instruction manual. None of us are perfect parents. We get some things right and miss it in other areas. We need to step back sometimes and remember that they have their own life, family, and choices to make. We can offer our advice, but if they choose differently, we should be respectful of their decisions and boundaries. If you have shown them the right path when they were young, rest in the fact that you've done a good job, and that God will lead and develop them as parents.

REFLECTIONS

+ Do you try to continue training your adult children even after they have left the nest?

+ From which areas of their lives do you need to take a step back and respect their boundaries?

ACTION OF THE WEEK

Write your adult children an apology note for times you did not respect their boundaries and tried to assert yourself as the parent. Ask for their forgiveness and assure them that they are doing a good job as parents.

GUIDED PRAYER

Father, continue to shape my character as a parent and/or grandparent. Give me grace and humility to know when I need to step back, and to offer my advice only when they ask for it. Amen.

I'm Your Friend, but I'm Also Your Parent

My son, pay attention to my wisdom,
turn your ear to my words of insight.

— *Proverbs 5:1*

COMMENTARY

As our children grow up and become adults, it is common to want to be their friend. Our relationship with them changes and matures, and it is normal to want to do adult things with them. When they are grown and have freedom of choice, we may fear that they won't want to spend time with us anymore, so in exchange for their friendship, we stop offering them wise instruction. It's easier to rationalize that we "did our job" as a parent, and now they are grown and are responsible for their own lives.

As our children grow, it is common for them to prioritize their relationships with their friends and shut out their parents. They can act like they are too cool for us; peer pressure enforces such behavior. If this has been the case with your children growing up, don't let rejection keep you from continuing to reach out to them with love and wise advice. It is most likely just a phase of their maturing process. If you stick with it, eventually they will realize for themselves that their friends might betray them or let them down, but your steadfast love and understanding will always be there.

Children don't come with instruction manuals, and parenting well doesn't always come naturally, but God has provided all the instructions in His Word, if we would only read it and do what it says. We know for sure, no matter how old our children get, a Christian parent's job is never done! God often speaks of His interactions not only with the individual, but with their descendants for several generations. Psalm 78:5–6 tells us, "For he issued his laws to Jacob; he gave his instructions to Israel. He commanded our ancestors to teach them to their children, so the next generation might know them—even the children not yet born, and they in turn will teach their own children." God places an expectation for us as parents to teach and lead our families so their faith holds forth in generations to come. Modeling a solid parent/child friendship will have untold benefits in years to come.

It is good to have a friendship with your adult children where they enjoy spending time with you and sharing their lives with you. That is truly a blessing! But never let that friendship take the place of sharing godly wisdom and direction with them and your grandchildren to come.

REFLECTIONS

✣ Has your relationship with your children developed into friendship as they became adults?

✣ If so, do you have a balance between being a friend and parent to them? Can you still share godly wisdom with them, and is it received?

ACTION OF THE WEEK

Reflect on and write down the ways you are either a friend to your adult children or the ways you can still speak into their lives as a parent. Have you found a balance between both?

GUIDED PRAYER

Father, I thank You because no matter how old I get, You will always be my friend and my Father. I sometimes get so wrapped up in parenting that I forget I am a child. Help me use Your great example to be as solid a parent as possible to my children and grandchildren to come. Amen.

Jesus Is Lord Over the Storms

The disciples went and woke him, saying, "Master,
Master, we're going to drown!" He got up and
rebuked the wind and the raging waters;
the storm subsided, and all was calm.

— Luke 8:24

COMMENTARY

Luke 8:22–25 gives an account of when the disciples and Jesus were in a boat. Jesus was asleep when a great storm arose. The huge waves were filling the boat with water, and the disciples, some experienced fishermen, were terrified. They woke Jesus up, shouting in fear that they were all about to drown. Jesus rebuked the storm with a command; the storm died down at once. Verse 25 reads, "Then he asked them, 'Where is your faith?' The disciples were terrified and amazed. 'Who is this man?' they asked each other. When he gives a command, even the wind and waves obey him!'"

Today we are no different than the disciples in the boat. When our adult children have not reached adult maturity, or they are bound by addictions, or are living out rebellious, selfish, and destructive behaviors, we can feel like our boat is sinking in a storm. We might be called upon to provide for their financial, emotional, and physical needs. Any and all of these categories can cause stress in our lives. Couple that with pressures from work, escalating bills, and waves in relationships, and you have a potential storm in the making. It would be nice if we as believers could nudge Jesus and have him calm our storm within seconds. Wouldn't it be great, since we place our faith in Jesus, if we never had to go through any storms in life? While this would be ideal, this is not realistic. Just as Jesus used the storm to teach the disciples about faith, He will use the storms in our lives, and in the lives of our children, to test our faith. It is in going through the storms with Him that our faith grows and matures.

If you are a believer and Jesus lives in you, He promises to never leave or forsake you. He won't promise us, or our children, a stormless life. But if He is "in your boat," you can rest assured that He won't let you drown. He is only allowing your faith to be tested. Keep your eyes on the Lord and He will carry you through!

REFLECTIONS

+ If you are experiencing the storms of life, where is your faith focused? Is it on the storm or on the answer—the Lord calming your storms?

+ What example do you set for your family during stormy times? Do they see you in faith or fear?

ACTION OF THE WEEK

Write down any "storms" you are facing, then write down a prayer over each one, giving them over to the Lord. You can trust him to calm your storms!

GUIDED PRAYER

Lord Jesus, help me set my focus on You and not on the storms around me. Allow me to trust You will calm them all. Amen.

Hope Deferred

Hope deferred makes the heart sick,
but a dream fulfilled is a tree of life.
— Proverbs 13:12

COMMENTARY

We all have hopes and dreams for our families. We hope that we have raised our children to confidently walk with God on their own. We hope that their lives and ours will be marked by God's protection and blessings. But what if those hopes and dreams are not manifesting? What do we do if our children are not walking with God but away from Him? These are cases of hope deferred.

When there seems to be no way to help, and no answer from God, we must cling to our faith. This may sound cliché, but it is the truth! That is what Abraham had to do. Romans 4:18 says even when there was no reason for hope, Abraham kept hoping—believing that he would become the father of many nations. He did not give unbelief a chance to discourage him.

Whatever it is that you are believing in God for, continue to pray in faith, expecting to see your dreams fulfilled. Hebrews 11:1 says faith is the confidence that what we hope for will actually happen; it gives us assurance about things we cannot see. Remembering the story from week 2 about the prodigal son (page 4), you will recall how I prayed for two years both for my son's protection and his safe return. I had no communication with him during that time, but I had constant communication with God. As I was praying one day for my son, the Lord had me read the story of the prodigal son three times until I grasped what He wanted me to see: a hopeful father watching expectantly for his son to return. That gave me the hope I needed to keep praying for his protection from the enemy, and from himself, until God did a work in my son, and the answer to my prayers showed up on my doorstep!

Hope is not a wishy-washy maybe. Hope is the concrete confidence that we hang on to. It is a rope anchored in the unseen promises and provision of God, which, if we cling to, we can have every expectation of receiving.

REFLECTIONS

* What hopes and dreams are you waiting to have fulfilled? Think about what you "really, really" wanted as a kid, and what you're hoping and dreaming for now. How different are they?

* In what ways have some of your hopes been brought to fruition? How does your faith allow you to know your future dreams will work out, too?

ACTION OF THE WEEK

Read the following verses on hope each morning, then write them down and meditate on them throughout the day to strengthen your belief: Psalm 33:20, Micah 7:7, Romans 4:18, and Romans 8:24–25.

GUIDED PRAYER

Father, give me an infusion of Your faith to keep on believing for my family, and help me place all my trust in you. Amen.

WEEK 18

Guard Your Heart

Above all else, guard your heart,
for everything you do flows from it.
— *Proverbs 4:23*

COMMENTARY

This week's verse encourages us to remind our adult children to think with their heart, not their head. The imagery of the word "guard" used here is that of an armed sentry at his post. It implies that what is being guarded is valuable. And it is: the object of the verse is your heart.

This is a peculiar verse, because we tend to think that most of our life decisions are made with our mind or intellect. As humans, we place a high value on making intelligent decisions; but this verse tells us otherwise. Proverbs was mostly written by King Solomon, son of David. He was known as the wisest man alive because, when given the opportunity to ask God for anything, he asked for a discerning heart to lead God's people. Because he asked for this and not wealth and long life, God gave it all to him. He ruled Israel in righteousness for forty years, but his humanness crept back in, and he started losing focus along the way, straying away from what God desired. He made decisions that were contrary to God's will for his life, and he made those bad decisions based on fleshly desires. He had many wives and concubines/mistresses, some from foreign nations, which God warned would usher in idolatry. The verse 1 Kings 11:4 says his wives turned his heart away, so that he built altars to worship foreign gods. He did not guard his heart, which led to his fall.

Our adult children will have to make many big decisions in their lives, from choosing a career path, to choosing a spouse, to making major financial decisions. It is natural for them to rely on their intellect and education to make the best choices. King Solomon, however, shows us to guard our hearts because we are to be guided by our faith-filled heart, and not our head. The lesson is shown throughout the Bible. God tells us that men look at outward appearances, according to man's intellect, but He looks at the heart (1 Samuel 16:7). And we are told that it is with the heart that man believes or activates their faith, not with the mind (Romans 10:10).

Proverbs 3:5–6 says that if we submit to God in all our ways, He will direct our paths. It tells us to trust in the Lord with all our heart, and not to lean on our own understanding or intellect. When it comes to making big decisions or major life choices, our adult children need to realize how important it is, as Christians, to keep our intentions and motives pure. The mind speaks intellect, but the heart speaks faith.

REFLECTIONS

+ What major life decisions—not just parenting related—have you made from the heart? Were they guided by faith and prayer far in advance?

+ When faced with future life decisions, what shifts do you need to make to lead with a faith-filled heart instead of an intellectual mind?

ACTION OF THE WEEK

The only way to guard your heart is through prayer. Make it a point to spend time this week praying specifically over your heart and your decisions, remembering that the heart speaks from a place of faith. Wisdom doesn't have to be a snap decision; it can be a result of dutiful, direct prayer.

GUIDED PRAYER

Lord, give me true wisdom and teach me how to better guard my heart and to trust You in all my ways. Amen.

The Lord Is My Shepherd

*Even though I walk through the valley of the shadow
of death, I will fear no evil, for you are with me;
your rod and your staff, they comfort me.*

— *Psalm 23:4 (ESV)*

COMMENTARY

Psalm 23 is one of the most often quoted chapters in the Bible. It
is read at many funerals because of the comfort it brings, and it
returns our focus to Jesus the Shepherd. I chose this topic because
a good friend of mine lost his adult son to addiction today. As
parents of adult children who are struggling, we often feel a sense
of guilt and failure. We might feel responsible for their struggles
but don't know what to do. Maybe we have tried everything we
can think of to help them. From church and prayer, to counseling,
to rehab; tough love to knock-down, drag-out battles; it's all for
them. We try our best but can only control our own actions, not the
actions of others. Sometimes the addiction takes our loved ones
from us prematurely.

What can you say or do when you see a friend grieving such a
tragic loss? I don't claim to have all the answers, but I do know the
Answer: His name is Jesus!

Verse 4 of this famous Psalm is key to setting our minds in the
right place. We all will walk through "the valley of the shadow
of death," but this verse says that the shepherd's rod and staff
"comfort me." What does that mean exactly?

The shepherd's rod was carried to fend off predators who would
attack the flock. It is a symbol of God's protection over us. The staff
was a long stick with a hooked end, used to guide the shepherd's
sheep when they veered off the path; the hook was used to rescue

them if they got entangled or fell in a ditch. The staff is a symbol that God is our guide and rescuer.

Maybe the best comfort we can take from this verse is to remember that He is with us in the valley. Sometimes the best thing we can do for a grieving friend is to remind them that we are with them, too, and we love them.

If you have lost an adult child to addiction or suicide, grief and sorrow are normal emotions. But please don't stay there, get help, whether it's with a pastor, counselor, or support group. Most of all, seek the Good Shepherd. He loves you deeply and walks with you.

(In memory of Nathan.)

REFLECTIONS

✣ Death is never easy to deal with, especially when you've lost someone close to you. How has God been your shepherd when you've grieved the loss of a loved one?

✣ What helped you most in the healing process?

ACTION OF THE WEEK

Make it a priority to learn ways to help someone struggling with addiction. Make a folder of resources you discover, and share it with those who need it.

GUIDED PRAYER

Father, comfort those who mourn the loss of a child as only You can. Show me how to be the friend they need in that moment. Amen.

The Tree Is Known by Its Fruit

Each tree is recognized by its own fruit. People do not pick figs from thornbushes, or grapes from briers.

— Luke 6:44

COMMENTARY

There are many examples in the Bible where people are compared to trees, in the sense that both are recognized by their fruit. Luke 6:45 elaborates on this idea and says, "A good man brings good things out of the good stored up in his heart, and an evil man brings evil things out of the evil stored up in his heart. For the mouth speaks what the heart is full of." As a tree is recognized by its fruit, so we will be known for what is produced out of the overflow of our heart (and mouth!).

The fruit that others see in you does not only reflect your character, but the fruit of your parenting will be seen in your children as well. As the father of three adult children, it is a blessing when someone else compliments the fruit of my tree. My youngest daughter and son-in-law hosted a parents' night out dinner that my wife and I usually host bimonthly. One of the parents that attended happened to be one of my wife's clients. He is a young father who is expecting his second daughter. He was very impressed with my daughter's grace and character. He said to her, "I have to meet the man that raised that young lady." I am a Christian Life Coach, so he booked a session with me, and we met at a coffee shop. He asked lots of great questions, and I shared what I had learned from raising two girls.

I am very proud of all my children, and I am blessed to know that they all love the Lord. Proverbs 17:6 says, "Children's children are a crown to the aged, and parents are the pride of their children."

My daughters are both expecting babies within a week of each other, and I can't wait to meet my new grandchildren and enjoy the fruit of their lives!

Seeing good fruit in the lives of your children is an indicator that the tree that produced them is good as well, but we can't take all the credit for the good fruit in our children's lives if we are constantly placing them in God's hands, watering them with His word, and loving them with the love we get from Him.

REFLECTIONS

✦ Is the fruit on your tree readily recognized as good fruit? During difficult times, can you still see the good fruit on your child's tree? (It's there!)

✦ What is the "fertilizer" that your tree needs to make its fruit even better?

ACTION OF THE WEEK

Make time this week to dote on the good fruit in your children's lives. Verbally compliment them at least twice as you "catch" them doing or sharing an example of the good that others (and you) see in them. For example: "I noticed how kindly you handled the shopper that knocked over your coffee. I don't think most people could have handled it that well, so thanks for setting a good example for others, too." It might feel awkward at first, if forthcoming praise is not your style, but it will get easier.

GUIDED PRAYER

Lord, may the tree of my life and the fruit that I bear bring You glory, and may it be pleasing in Your sight. Amen.

Heavenly Perspectives

*And God raised us up with Christ and seated us
with him in the heavenly realms in Christ Jesus.*

— *Ephesians 2:6*

COMMENTARY

This is a strange verse to ponder as it is written in the past tense, as a thing that has already transpired. How can that be true? After all, we are still down here on Earth, working, playing, and living our lives, right? What are we to learn from this verse? In its context, we can see from the two previous verses that, in God's perspective, we are already seated with Him in Heaven! Verses 4–5 read: "But because of his great love for us, God, who is rich in mercy, made us alive with Christ even when we were dead in transgressions—it is by grace you have been saved." This whole passage is written in the past tense and is telling us that in his mind, it's as good as done!

We are not avatars in some alternate dimension, so what are we to make of this? I believe He told us this so that we can live each day down here with a heavenly perspective; to see things and people the way God sees them, and to act accordingly. This is anything but natural; it is completely supernatural! We as believers have been given the unique ability to view our circumstances, our marriages, and our interactions with our adult children from a heavenly perspective. It is natural to believe in what we can see, but it requires faith from God to live our lives according to His word, His promises, and His perspective because He is the only one who knows what the future holds.

Too many of us professing Christianity live and parent from an earthly, human perspective. Giving our adult children what they earn or deserve is natural. An earthly, carnal perspective withholds forgiveness and mercy until it is earned. The heavenly perspective loves and forgives others because we have been forgiven so much ourselves. Earthly grace is very limited, but from the heavenly perspective grace overflows and abounds. Learning to see others, even our enemies, with God's eyes, and treat them the way He has treated us, will set an example for your adult children to follow that will change the world around them and bless both of you with eternal treasures.

REFLECTIONS

+ In what ways does your perspective need to shift from an earthly one to a heavenly one? Do you think it will be easy?

+ What degree of revelation do you have concerning this verse? How can you gain more understanding?

ACTION OF THE WEEK

Spend some time in prayer contemplating and writing down areas of your life that need a shift in perspective. Is it work, a romantic relationship, parenting, general life priorities? Create a plan to work on some shifting, starting today.

GUIDED PRAYER

Father, teach me to see and treat others the way You do. Teach me how to live my life from Heaven to earth. Amen.

When Your Relationships Are Tested

*By faith Abraham, when God tested him, offered Isaac
as a sacrifice. He who had embraced the promises
was about to sacrifice his one and only son.*

— *Hebrews 11:17*

COMMENTARY

In Genesis 22 we find a crazy story about how God told Abraham to
sacrifice his only son Isaac. This jolting story will likely incite lots
of questions in the mind of the believer. We are not told exactly how
old Isaac was when he was almost sacrificed by his own father, but
we are given a clue that he was not a little boy. In verse 6 we read
that Isaac carried all the wood for the burnt offering up the moun-
tain. This seems to indicate that he was likely either late teens or
early twenties, making him an adult child. I can't think of a worse
scenario that would test a parent/adult child relationship. Talk
about needing counseling!

At one awkward moment in their journey Isaac said to his
dad, "We have the wood, the knife, and the fire, but where is the
sacrifice?" Abraham simply answered, "The Lord will provide a
sacrifice." After his dad built the altar, placed the wood, and got
everything prepared, you can feel the tension in the relationship.
Abraham then bound his only son, placed him on the altar, and
was about to carry out the unthinkable when God stopped him and
told him not to lay a hand on the boy. Instead, Abraham sacrificed a
ram caught in a nearby thicket. The last verse of this story says that
Abraham returned to his servants and they left for Beersheba, but it

doesn't mention Isaac at all. I can imagine him running as far away from his dad as possible!

We tend to think that this test was unique to Abraham, but think about how Isaac's faith was tested, not only in His God but in his own father as well. Isaac saw that his dad was a man deeply faithful to the Lord (more faithful than Isaac perhaps expected!). Though we will never face a test like this, we will definitely have our relationships tested from time to time. There should be an inherent level of trust between the parent and child, and while this is not always the case, children typically trust their own parents. They don't usually worry about the bills, taxes, or dinner, because that is the parents' job. Their job is just to trust and obey. So it is to be in our relationship with our heavenly Father.

REFLECTIONS

+ Think about how your own relationships with your adult children have been tested. Was your own faith in God being tested as well? What about theirs? In what ways?

+ What was the outcome of the test? What did you learn? How did you grow?

ACTION OF THE WEEK

Read the whole story of Abraham and Isaac in Genesis 22. If you have the time, read a few different Bible translations to compare phrases and word choices. Write down your thoughts, feelings, and questions that arise about the story.

GUIDED PRAYER

Thank You, Father, that my faith will never be tested as Abraham! I ask Your forgiveness for any tests that I have failed, and ask for Your grace to pass any and all future tests with increasing faith and trust in You. Amen.

Co-Parenting

> *"Why were you searching for me?" he asked.*
> *"Didn't you know I had to be in my Father's house?"*
> — *Luke 2:49*

COMMENTARY

The Bible doesn't really give us any stories or parables on co-parenting, but it does provide one glimpse in a story about Jesus as a boy being raised by Joseph and Mary. It is found in Luke 2:41–52, and it describes how, while on a journey, Joseph and Mary actually lost the Son of God!

I have twenty-five years of co-parenting experience, and while my oldest daughter, Abigail, and I have a great relationship now, it hasn't always been easy. Her birth father and I could not be more different. Let's just say that he didn't agree with me in most areas, including discipline. The one thing we did share was our deep love for Abigail. She was only a year old when I met her mother, and when she was two, I was her stepdad. We have had the usual bumps in the road that most natural parents have with their child, but things were relatively "normal" as she grew.

When Abby graduated high school, she chose to attend a Bible training school in Alabama. Her birth dad got to load her stuff in his truck, drive her there, and help her get settled in. I was a bit jealous but dealing with it. He came outside while loading the truck, and he thanked me for being the dad that he wasn't able to be for her, and he said that he was very proud of who she had grown to be because of her mother and me. I was shocked, humbled, and honored by his gracious words. It was one of the most compassionate things a co-parent could do!

When Abby met the man she would marry, and they started planning their wedding, I wondered who would walk her down the aisle. Who would give her hand in marriage? She pleasantly surprised me and showed me that there is still room for two dads in her life. She arranged for her dad to walk her down the aisle and for me to officiate the wedding (which I did with much pride and joy!). When we raise our kids with respect to the other set of parents, there is room for both sets to respectfully remain in their lives at the same time.

If you are a stepparent, I want to encourage you to love and treat your child like they are your own, even when it's difficult. Never stop pursuing a deeper relationship with them.

REFLECTIONS

✢ Parenting is hard; co-parenting is even harder. You need the love, wisdom, and grace of God in your life to be good at it. How do you invite Him in when you need help?

✢ What areas of your co-parenting relationships need some work? Is it with the child or the other parents?

ACTION OF THE WEEK

Through a card or conversation, tell the other parents some of the good qualities you see in them, and a specific, positive effect you see they've had on your child(ren). They too have been challenged with the job of co-parenting. Appreciation or acknowledgment from you will mean a lot.

GUIDED PRAYER

Father, help my children and/or stepchildren forgive my shortcomings, and help me to better show them how much I love them. Amen.

Controlled Friction

As iron sharpens iron, so one person sharpens another.

— *Proverbs 27:17*

COMMENTARY

Friction is the energy created by rubbing two opposing objects against each other. Have you ever heard the phrase "That person rubs me the wrong way"? It isn't referring to a bad massage; it usually implies conflict and irritation. Conflict is unavoidable in life, but it is manageable if we can learn to control the friction.

There are lessons to be learned from the process of sharpening a knife or tool. The process involves grinding away rough material with an abrasive object in a repeated, controlled manner, with the intended goal of refining the edge. There are different tools we can use to sharpen as well, such as a grinding wheel, a sanding belt, a diamond coated steel, or a whetstone. One of the oldest and best methods is the whetstone and honing oil. After applying the oil to the surface of the stone, the person rubs the blade against the stone in repetitions and with a controlled angle until the desired sharpness is achieved. Then the edge can be polished to razor sharpness.

When confronting our adult children, we must remember that not all conflict is bad. If it can be controlled and harnessed, it can actually be beneficial for both people. The first step is to take control of the situation by choosing words and questions to steer or guide the conversation. It's like picking the tool you're going to use to sharpen your knife. Where do you want this conversation to lead and end? What words or phrases can you use that you know your child will hear? What phrases or words will they block out? Are there parts of the past to avoid completely (for now)?

Next, envision your carefully chosen words and speak them slowly, to remove the object of contention. This is like placing the edge of the knife onto the stone to smooth the roughness. Don't forget the oil that helps it all go (literally) smoothly! The honing oil here is symbolic of the Holy Spirit. Apply the oil by pausing to invite the Holy Spirit into the conflict. He can help refine both of you into sharper and more useful people.

Now it's time to "polish the edge." Your kids aren't going to want to continue to talk to you if they know your knife edge is out and ready to cut. Let them know it's safe to talk to you. Whenever you need it, add back in the oil of the Holy Spirit!

REFLECTIONS

✠ Conflict is an unavoidable fact of life. If you have any human contact at all, you will face it. How can you better learn to control those parent-child conflict moments to make them beneficial?

✠ Which child relationships in your life can use some sharpening? Are you causing the friction in the relationship, or are they? What role do you play in the process and how can you hone your knife?

ACTION OF THE WEEK

Begin by praying and asking the Holy Spirit to show you how to refine yourself and your relationships through controlled friction. Write down the words, thoughts, or mental pictures you receive from Him, and begin the process.

GUIDED PRAYER

Lord, as I yield to Your refinement in my life, help me be a useful tool in Your hand to refine my relationships. Amen.

The Power of Agreement

Do two walk together unless they have agreed to do so?

— Amos 3:3

COMMENTARY

We make agreements several times a day, maybe even hundreds. From what to put on, to what's for dinner, to stopping at a red light. Agreements are the actions we take and the choices we make based on a decision of our will. The fact that man has free will is evident on nearly every, if not every, page of the Bible. We make so many agreements per day that we seldom give them much thought at all. On weightier matters like major purchases or life-impacting events, we approach them slowly and take them seriously. When written down and signed by both parties, agreements become a formal, legally binding contract.

There is such a mighty, powerful force contained in the exercise of agreements, that they can be both a blessing and a curse, and it all hinges on our own free will, our choice. Scary thought to ponder! Romans 10:10 says, "For with the heart one believes unto righteousness, and with the mouth confession is made unto salvation." The Greek word for confession means to agree with. Our agreements are made by exercising our free will and they are ratified by our words.

We need to examine our lives to see what we are in agreement with: Truth or lies? Life or death? Blessing or cursing? Faith or fear? The severity of our agreements was demonstrated by Adam and Eve when they fell out of agreement with God and, by the exercise of their will, came into agreement with Satan, and sin and death entered the world by their actions.

We must reconcile our own agreements and then teach this principle to our children, and especially adult children, so that they will be equipped to make good and right decisions. They need to be taught the magnitude of the power of their agreements, so they will take them as seriously as they truly are. Jesus said that "everyone will have to give account on the day of judgment for every empty word they have spoken. For by your words you will be acquitted, and by your words you will be condemned" (Matthew 12:36–37).

REFLECTIONS

+ What are some major agreements your child got to observe you making (for example: buying a car, divorce, adoption, moving to a new town) when they were younger? Do you think they saw a rash decision maker or one who thought about the pros and cons before committing to an answer? What do you think they learned from it?

+ What agreements do you see evident in your children's lives, good or bad?

ACTION OF THE WEEK

Take inventory of the agreements in your life, both good and bad, and write them in two columns. Pray over and verbally break off and nullify your bad agreements and ratify the good ones.

GUIDED PRAYER

God give me clarity as I look inward, and show me what agreements I need to break off of my life and then those of my family as well. Amen.

Vulnerability

But he said to me, "My grace is sufficient for you, for my power is made perfect in weakness." Therefore I will boast all the more gladly about my weaknesses, so that Christ's power may rest on me.

— *2 Corinthians 12:9*

COMMENTARY

One night while having dinner with my three young children, my oldest daughter (around 10 at the time) asked me if I had ever done drugs. I hesitated to answer because I didn't think they were mature enough to have that discussion. She said, "You hesitated, so that means you have." But I hesitated because I feared that answering honestly at that time could damage how my children saw me. I felt pressure to be vulnerable, and I didn't like it one bit.

Most people have issues with vulnerability. There are many reasons for this, including past hurts, abuse, and trauma. It brings to the surface feelings of insecurity, weakness, and failure, so we tend to avoid it all together. It's especially hard for those men who are raised with the belief that men are to be strong and not show weakness. We tend to build up walls around our weaknesses and wounds, guarding them closely. After all, we have read Proverbs 4:23, which tells us to guard our heart because everything we do flows from it. Taking this out of context, we can validate building walls and defenses around our hearts, not allowing others access. The problem with this is that, over time, our hearts get calloused and hard. For instance, Jesus said, "For this people's heart has become calloused; they hardly hear with their ears, and they have closed their eyes. Otherwise they might see with their eyes, hear with their ears, understand with their hearts and turn, and I would heal them" (Matthew 13:15).

It is a difficult thing to admit our faults, weaknesses, and failures to others, but if we want our relationships to grow and develop, we have to learn to let down our guard and open up to those closest to us. This includes our spouses, our close friends, and yes, even our children. If we can be honest with our adult children and tell them about our faults, we set an example for them to open up and let others in as well. It opens the door to confession, repentance, and forgiveness. This is the key to freedom! James 5:16 tells us, "Therefore confess your sins to each other and pray for each other so that you may be healed. The prayer of a righteous person is powerful and effective." If we can be vulnerable and honest with our children about our weaknesses as parents, it paves the way for their healing and freedom as well.

REFLECTIONS

- What walls need to come down from around our hearts so they can begin to heal?

- Are you vulnerable with God, your spouse, and your child(ren)? Do they have full access to your heart?

ACTION OF THE WEEK

Surely your child has gone through or is going through a rough patch similar to one you've experienced. You might have made good decisions or not so good ones; either way, you learned a thing or two. Make time to have a vulnerable discussion with your adult children about your past, to open the door for deeper honesty and discussion with them. Watch the healing process begin.

GUIDED PRAYER

Lord, You said Your power is made perfect in weakness. Help me be vulnerable and open with those I love. Amen.

Dealing with Anxiety, Part 1

When anxiety was great within me,
your consolation brought me joy.

— *Psalm 94:19*

COMMENTARY

According to the Anxiety and Depression Association of America, in 2020, anxiety disorders were the most common mental illness in the United States. They affect 40 million adults (age 18 and older)—18.1 percent of the population—every year. Anxiety is highly treatable, yet their study shows less than 40 percent of sufferers receive treatment. Their website also says, "It's not uncommon for someone with an anxiety disorder to also suffer from depression or vice versa. Nearly one-half of those diagnosed with depression are also diagnosed with an anxiety disorder."

Parenting adult children can be a cause for elevated stress and anxiety, especially if they are exhibiting self-destructive behaviors. Whether they are playing video games all day instead of looking for work, acting defiantly toward you, or just living an ungodly lifestyle, parents are sure to have elevated anxiety levels.

If you are taking prescription anxiety medications, that is not a bad thing. It is the most common form of relief sought by millions like you. However, as believers, we have access to the Great Physician Jesus! He not only cares about your spiritual well-being, but he also wants to take away your anxiety, worries, and fear. In 1 Peter 5:7 it says, "Cast all your anxiety on him because he cares for you." You may be thinking, "I've tried that and it didn't work." I want you to think of it like fishing. If you are like me, you may cast over and over only to get hung up on something on the bottom and have to start all over. Fishing can be discouraging, until you finally get that first catch.

After that first catch, your joy and resolve to keep going is renewed. It is the same principle in prayer. Jesus said, "Ask and it will be given to you; seek and you will find; knock and the door will be opened to you" (Matthew 7:7).

Philippians tells us, rather than feeling anxious, to offer prayer and petition (and thanksgiving of course!) to God. Hang in there, Mom and Dad; the answers will come if you pray with patient but persistent expectation. Know that taking medication is not antithetical to faith in prayer. Keep taking it if prescribed, and place your faith in God's desire and ability to heal and restore.

REFLECTIONS

- Anxiety is common to us all. It becomes a disorder when it prevents us from handling normal, everyday duties. Yet any level of anxiety can be crippling and unmanageable at times. How we deal with it will determine how severe it becomes and how long it lasts. What have you done recently to help ease anxiety?

- Medical treatment is not a bad option, but remember to seek God first for your remedy. He will guide you toward the best treatment path for you.

ACTION OF THE WEEK

If you are struggling with anxiety and worry, practice casting your cares on Him, and if possible, do it while casting a line in the water as well! (I find fishing to be a great meditative way to be at peace, while feeling the constant, quiet presence of the Lord.) Try any kind of outdoor activity this week.

GUIDED PRAYER

Lord, I believe Your word, that You care for me and don't want me to carry the weight of anxiety. Please renew my resolve to ask, seek, and knock until the answer comes. Amen.

Dealing with Anxiety, Part 2

*Do not be anxious about anything, but in every
situation, by prayer and petition, with thanksgiving,
present your requests to God.*

— *Philippians 4:6*

COMMENTARY

As we have read in part 1, anxiety is a major issue that affects tens
of millions of people in the United States alone, not to mention
globally. It can be so debilitating that hearing someone say to pray
about it may sound like a simplistic and insincere response, but I
want you to grasp the real power in prayer! Praying does not mean
begging God to do this or that for us. There are examples in scripture for us to follow, all of which involve asking in faith or with
expectant hope.

God showed me a long time ago that the prayer of thanksgiving
was an important aspect of praying in faith. As I read and pondered
Philippians 4:6, the words "with thanksgiving" stood out to me.
The verse says that, when dealing with anxiety, we should not only
pray and petition God but also pray with thanksgiving when we ask.
It doesn't make natural sense to say thank you *before* we receive
the answer. But the kingdom of God is antithetical to the carnal,
natural way of thinking. We are taught from an early age to say
thank you after someone gives us something, not before, but God is
looking for faith in our prayers.

Faith is believing in something we don't already see, so praying
in faith means we are trusting that God hears us and will answer
us. In Mark 11:24 Jesus spoke about this kind of prayer. He said,
"Therefore I tell you, whatever you ask for in prayer, believe that

you have received it, and it will be yours." In other words, saying thank you when we pray is the same as saying "it's as good as done!"

While you are casting your cares on Jesus, and praying over and for your adult children, practice saying thank you as you ask, seek, and knock. As weird as it may seem at first, try to believe that you have already received the answers. After all, it was Jesus who said to pray that way! I believe that God can hear and answer any type of prayer, but it works even better when we pray the way our Lord has taught us.

REFLECTIONS

- ✦ Taking your anxiety and worries to the Lord in prayer should not be a last resort; it should be our first response. Do you often pray first about something worrisome, or is it your last option? It might take practice to flip the order around.

- ✦ Learning to pray the prayer of thanksgiving can be strange to us, but if we are open to learning and applying what we read in scripture, we will see greater success.

ACTION OF THE WEEK

Try saying thank you as you pray this week. How does it feel? Does it get easier? Keep a journal of your answered prayers.

GUIDED PRAYER

Thank You, Father, for teaching me new ways to pray in faith! I also thank You for relieving my anxiety as I cast my cares upon You. Amen.

Busyness

"You expected much, but see, it turned out to be little. What you brought home, I blew away. Why?" declares the LORD Almighty. "Because of my house, which remains a ruin, while each of you is busy with your own house."

— *Haggai 1:9*

COMMENTARY

As I was pondering this topic, a 1974 song by Harry Chapin came to mind. It's titled "Cat's in the Cradle," and it is all about a dad who was absent as his son grew up because the dad was too busy working. The song ends with the son all grown up. When the dad retires, he wants to spend time with his son, but the son is too busy; he grew up to be just like his dad.

Sometimes our children grow into adults and leave home never to return. Maybe they chose a college or career path that takes them far from home. Perhaps they joined the military and their service takes them around the world. Or one bad reason might be that they grew up in a dysfunctional home or had strained or harmful relationships at home. When they grow up, they go out on their own to make a new life for themselves and have no desire to go back home and subject themselves to such relationships.

We cannot make our adult children want to spend time with us. Sometimes their busyness is not intentional; it may just be work or school related. What we can do is continue to pursue a relationship with them, letting them know that we love them and always welcome them back home. In doing so, we should avoid overdoing it in our pursuit. This may push them further away and justify their reasons for leaving.

It is always okay to pray for them, though! You can do this as often as you like with no backlash from them. Pray for their protection, peace, healing of the heart, and pray for the Lord to restore the relationship. If you are the reason for their avoidance that is disguised as busyness, pray for your own healing as well, and work to resolve the underlying issues in you, so you can hopefully have a good relationship again.

If your adult children seem too busy to make time for you, maybe it's best to let them go without "chasing" them. Try not to let your feelings affect the way you interact with them when they do call or come around. When you get to spend that rare time together, try to let them take the lead on what to do or what to talk about.

REFLECTIONS

+ We're all busy. But it's never a good thing to be too busy for loved ones. If we don't have the time for them, we need to make the time for them. How often are you in contact with your adult children? Do they still make time for you?

+ What is within your power to change about your relationship with your children? Are you ready to start doing it?

ACTION OF THE WEEK

There are probably a hundred different things we wish we did differently while parenting our children when they were younger. If we only knew then what we know now! Since we can't change the past, and "what ifs" get us nowhere but frustrated, let's look ahead. Think of ways you can redeem lost time in your children's lives, and then do it!

GUIDED PRAYER

Father, forgive me if I have neglected my relationship with You. Help me prioritize my close family relationships to make them the best they can be. Amen.

Renewing Your Mind

Do not conform to the pattern of this world, but be transformed by the renewing of your mind. Then you will be able to test and approve what God's will is— his good, pleasing and perfect will.

— *Romans 12:2*

COMMENTARY

Do you or your adult child often compare yourselves to others, wondering if you are normal? Do you take constructive criticism as a personal attack? Do you or your child seek the approval of others but find it difficult to receive a compliment? Are you living out what others have said about you as a child?

If you answered yes to these, you may be an adult child emotionally, even though you are a parent of adult children. Our self-image is often shaped by our childhood, and if we never correct the negative self-image others have imposed on us, it will affect the way we see ourselves as adults.

When I was a child, I felt different from other children at an early age. I am left-handed and colorblind. I had elementary teachers who tried to correct my left handedness, and I was teased by other kids for being colorblind most of my childhood. As an adult, I have come to understand that left-handed people learn and process differently than right-handed people. But back then, if I didn't understand what the teacher was teaching when most of the class did, I was called dumb and stupid.

It is a fact that only about 10 percent of the world is left-handed, and roughly 4.5 percent are colorblind. There are also several studies that show a higher diagnosis of ADD/ADHD in both of these categories. Being affected by both contributed even more to my feeling very different from others. As a result, I was held back in the fourth grade, and my childhood self-image was extremely low. This carried over into adulthood as extreme defensiveness and an emotional need for acceptance affecting my relationships with my wife, children, and friends.

It wasn't until I started learning what God has to say about my identity in Christ that I started to correct some of the wrong mindsets. This week's verse describes the renewing of the mind, or changing our thinking for the better. In fact, the Greek word repent means to have a change of thought.

Only through the renewing of our minds as adult parents will we be able to help our adult children heal as well.

REFLECTIONS

+ How have childhood wounds and negative words affected your adult self-image and emotional responses? Are you ready to heal those wounds?

+ What wrong thinking needs to be renewed in your identity?

ACTION OF THE WEEK

If you could speak to your childhood self, what would you say to encourage yourself and change your self-image? Write a letter to yourself as a child, replacing the lies you believed about yourself with truth. Remind your younger self that no matter how you were raised or what went on, you were and *are* loved.

GUIDED PRAYER

Father, teach me through Your word about my identity. Show me how Your word can change the way I see myself through the process of learning how You see me. I want to be healed myself, so I can help my adult children heal as well, amen.

The Root of Bitterness

*See to it that no one falls short of the grace of
God and that no bitter root grows up to cause
trouble and defile many.*

— Hebrews 12:15

COMMENTARY

Jack was my father-in-law for 24 years. He had three children from
a previous marriage: Melanie, Missy, and Jeff. He would later marry
my wife's mother. His son, Jeff, was very angry with him for divorc-
ing his mother, and he never forgave Jack. He allowed that anger to
go unchecked, and it sprouted as a root of bitterness that grew up
to trouble him and cause grief in the family. I remember early in my
marriage going to Missy's wedding, which was the only time I ever
saw Jeff. He would not speak to or even make eye contact with Jack,
or anyone else in the family for that matter. The bitterness he carried and apparently nurtured for over 30 years had kept him from
ever being able to restore his relationship with his father.

When Jack's health had deteriorated and he was at the end of his
life, Jeff was told that his father would not be with us much longer.
Instead of going to see his dad and make amends, he clung to that
bitter root to the end. I'm sure that bitterness remains even today.
It has damaged his relationships with both of his sisters as well. Job
21:25 says, "Another dies in bitterness of soul, never having enjoyed
anything good." It is a great tragedy to spend your life harboring
bitterness and unforgiveness, never really enjoying happiness and
relationships with family.

Hebrews 12:15 warns us of the danger and poison that a root
of bitterness will bring to our lives. But it also tells us to look after
each other, and that the antidote is the grace of God.

Maybe a rift with one of your adult children is going on right now. Have you allowed the poisonous root of bitterness to grow in your heart? The only time it is too late to uproot it is when death severs our chances of restoration. It's time to start weeding. The first step is to receive God's grace and forgiveness to heal your own heart, and then extend the olive branch to those with whom you want to see your relationship restored.

REFLECTIONS

- Pain and inner wounds can affect our lives in many ways and, if they are not dealt with, can devastate and ultimately destroy our lives. How has pain affected you? Bitterness might have been festering a long time, becoming so much a part of your daily life that you don't even realize it's there.

- How could you initiate the removal of the root of bitterness with your adult child?

ACTION OF THE WEEK

Like weeding a garden, removing poisonous weeds in our hearts involves work. Resolve yourself to allow the grace of God to work in your life. Ask Him to guide you to the specific source of your pain or bitterness, and for His help on yanking those weeds and letting them go. Extend an arm of peace and forgiveness to those you love.

GUIDED PRAYER

Lord, I need your grace and mercy in my life in greater measure. I invite you to uproot any bitterness or unforgiveness from my heart, and I trust you to restore my broken relationships. Amen.

How to Forgive and Forget

For a son dishonors his father, a daughter rises up
against her mother, a daughter-in-law against
her mother-in-law—a man's enemies are the
members of his own household.

— *Micah 7:6*

COMMENTARY

Too often, family bonds are damaged and broken by offenses committed by another family member, and unforgiveness divides the home. As Christians, we are commanded to forgive others. I have heard, and even taught in the past, that God is the only one who can forgive and forget our sins. While we humans might forgive others when they sin against us, we rarely forget the wrong done to us. We tend to define "forget" as to lose remembrance of or to be unable to recall something, like forgetting a name or where we placed our car keys. But according to Merriam-Webster's Dictionary, there is another meaning to the word forget, which is to intentionally disregard or overlook. The key to forgetting is to intentionally disregard and overlook the sins committed against us. Okay, it's not that simple, but it is doable.

You may be familiar with the story of Joseph, a son of Jacob, in the Old Testament. Joseph was an adult child who was mistreated by his brothers and sold into slavery because of their jealousy and anger toward him. He was later falsely accused and thrown into prison, lied about, and forsaken by all but God. Despite all that he endured at the hand of his brothers, Joseph is the perfect picture of forgiving and forgetting. Joseph named his firstborn Manasseh, which means in Hebrew "to cause to forget." He said, "It is because

God has made me forget all my trouble and all my father's household." It wasn't that he couldn't remember how evil his own brothers treated him; it was because God caused him to intentionally overlook their sins against him. I think he named his firstborn "forget" because he needed a daily reminder that he had a choice to intentionally overlook the past. Joseph named his second son Ephraim which means "twice as blessed."

In the end, it doesn't really matter who wronged us or if we feel as though one of our children betrayed us. Withholding forgiveness is like drinking poison hoping the offender will get sick. Forgiveness releases us from the bitterness and resentment that can destroy our lives. It doesn't mean we are saying the transgression is "okay," only that we are releasing the grip it holds on us. We are choosing to forget. To forget the sins of others against us opens the windows of Heaven for us to receive a double blessing!

REFLECTIONS

* Are you withholding forgiveness from your children? If so, why? Does it help to think of forgiveness as a release from the pain it caused you, as opposed to an acceptance of the action?

* With God's help you can not only forgive but also be doubly blessed if you choose to forget.

ACTION OF THE WEEK

Pray for God to show you who you still need to forgive. Write down their names, and then through your own choice to be obedient, release them from their sins. It's a blessing you'll be giving yourself!

GUIDED PRAYER

Father, I truly want to walk in forgiveness toward others. Help me not only forgive but choose to forget the past. Amen.

Children, Obey Your Parents

Children, obey your parents in the Lord, for this is right.
— *Ephesians 6:1*

COMMENTARY

This verse is short and to the point. It sounds a lot like "just do it because I said so." Parents love to use that line as often as possible, because it removes any room for debate or protest. When your children are small, that phrase might work for a while, but as they get older, they will push the boundaries and question the rules. This is normal human behavior—you probably did it, too.

If we continue reading Ephesians 6, we discover that it is in reference to one of the Ten Commandments. Verse 2 says, "Honor your father and mother," and verse 3 gives the why: "If you honor your father and mother, 'things will go well for you, and you will have a long life on the earth.'"

Obedience is one lesson every child must learn. To make it very far in the world, they often need to obey authority figures and rules like traffic laws. Doing so can keep them safe and maintain civil order.

When your grown children come back home, for whatever reason, rules will be one of the first conversations you will have. The old dynamics have changed; you aren't going to ground your child if they don't comply. The consequence now might be that they are no longer welcome to stay there if certain rules are broken.

It can be difficult to balance between grace and justice, but walk that line you must. I had to at one point, when our oldest son moved back home, for the third time, because he was struggling with alcoholism and depression. I explained from the start that his stay with us was contingent on him wanting to get better, and that

I would not tolerate lying. We knew the rules had to get stricter and the repercussions more severe. When our rules were repeatedly violated, as hard as it was, I had no other choice but to tell him he had to leave.

This is very difficult and painful to do as a loving parent, but the obedience of the child is a must if they want to see the blessings attached to it. That part about "things will go well for you, and you will have a long life on the earth"—that isn't just a good suggestion. It is the second part of that commandment. It's God's Word!

REFLECTIONS

+ Are your house rules fair, and have they been clearly articulated from the start? Do the same rules apply to everyone?

+ What is the breaking point, the part of the rule that if broken ends the agreement?

ACTION OF THE WEEK

If you have adult children living with you, assess and evaluate your rules of the house.

What rules need to be changed? What rules need to be enforced? If you do not have adult children living with you, evaluate with your significant other how well or not so well you did on making and enforcing rules as you parented. Are there rules you should create or enforce now, regardless of living situation?

GUIDED PRAYER

Father God, show me areas of my life where I have not been obedient to Your word, and help me realign my will with Yours. Amen.

Commitment Is a Roller Coaster

One who has unreliable friends soon comes to ruin,
but there is a friend who sticks closer than a brother.
— *Proverbs 18:24*

COMMENTARY

I remember my very first rollercoaster ride. It was the Shockwave at Six Flags in Arlington, Texas, and I was 14 years old. I was terrified. The line was long, and my friend asked me to wait through the line with him. He said we could talk until it was his turn to ride, and I could walk down the ramp and wait for him. We got to talking and cutting up, and the next thing I knew, I was sitting in the second car and the safety harness was latched down onto me. I was now committed to the ride, come what may. I thought I might fall out at any moment, so I clung to that safety bar for dear life. But as soon as it was over, I was running to get back in the line. When I let go of fear and embraced the ride, I found it to be one of my favorite theme park rides of all.

Having a relationship with your adult children can feel much the same as a roller coaster. It can often cause the same symptoms, like dizziness, nausea, and fear. There are some twists and turns and loops involved in the relationship, peaks and valleys where things can go unexpectedly or not as planned, and it can feel like things are going crazy and you might fly off the rails. A committed parent sits in the car next to their grown child and says, "I am in this with you to the end." They cling to the safety bar that is God and experience every twist and turn of the ride together. The adult child needs the security of that kind of commitment, like riding a roller coaster next to a friend who has done it before and can reassure them that they are safe.

Another similarity between this relationship and roller coasters is that after a few rides, your confidence grows and you allow yourself to experience the exhilaration of letting go and raising your hands. You will only experience this when you let go of fear. If our children see us letting go and raising our hands (trusting in and praising God), they will be inspired to do the same, resulting in them conquering their own fears and experiencing new joys along the ride.

REFLECTIONS

* How does this story and verse relate to you and your adult children? Were you initially petrified at the idea of becoming a parent?

* How have your own ups and downs affected their lives? How has sitting by their side on the roller coaster of their life felt for them and you?

ACTION OF THE WEEK

Share this topic with your own grown children and discuss any roller coaster, theme park, hike, swim, class trip/presentation, or other adventurous time you have shared—a time when they were afraid but it worked out fine. Did they sense you were sitting beside them the whole time (literally or figuratively), holding on to the safety bar that is God?

GUIDED PRAYER

Thank You, Lord, for all my parenting experiences, both the ups and downs, and twists and turns, as they helped shape our family. Help me continue to express willingness to sit by my child's side. Amen.

This Little Light of Mine

In the same way, let your light shine before others,
that they may see your good deeds and glorify
your Father in heaven.

— *Matthew 5:16*

COMMENTARY

One of my favorite vacations as a family was our trip to Puerto Rico. Our children were getting older, and it was an opportunity to make some memories of a lifetime with them. One evening we booked a night kayaking tour. We all paddled down a stretch of coastline for about a half mile and entered into what is called a "bio bay" for the unique experience of swimming in a warm lagoon with billions of tiny dinoflagellates. These microscopic plankton reproduce and then die off only when stirred by a fish, a kayak paddle, or a swimmer. The most incredible part is that they emit a bioluminescence, causing the water and everything around them to glow. Our kids were in absolute awe. It was such a pleasure to share that with them and see the amazement in their eyes.

There is a similarity between these fascinating creatures and the children of God. We have the light of the world deposited inside each of us, and as we interact in love with one another, that light starts to seep out of us in ways that makes us almost appear to glow. As we then allow the love of God to flow through us to others, they will see the light in and on us and hopefully want to know where they can get it. Love is the most powerful force in the universe, and it is highly contagious!

Another thing I got to do was enjoy a round of golf with my son. The golf course was a tropical paradise complete with large iguanas roaming it. We had a great time playing a game we both love, and we shared a bonding moment that we will both remember for years to come. His brain is wired much the same as mine, and I understand him and can relate to him on many levels. As we played the game, I got to see much of myself in him. But I also see the light of our Heavenly Father in him, and it brings a joy and a light to my heart that I cherish.

I cannot think of a greater joy as a parent than seeing the light and love of God shine in the hearts and lives of your children. Watching them light up the world around them, and then starting to see that light spread to their own children is amazing, stirring deep gratitude to the Father for His perfect love shining in us.

REFLECTIONS

✦ In what ways have you seen the glow of God in your children? Do/did they realize it's the light of Him emanating from inside them?

✦ Now that your children are adults, do they still let that glow shine? When was the last time you saw the sparkle of Jesus in their eyes?

ACTION OF THE WEEK

Encourage and appreciate your adult children by telling them three ways you see God's light shining through them. Maybe it's how they run a faith-filled home, make helping others a priority, or see the positive when others see the negative. They will love to hear it!

GUIDED PRAYER

Thank You, Father, for placing Your love in our hearts. Let it burn bright in me and my children so that others can see what You have done in our lives. Amen.

Controlling Your Temper

"In your anger do not sin": Do not let the sun go down while you are still angry.

— *Ephesians 4:26*

COMMENTARY

Anger is a heated emotion we all experience from time to time. Anger is not a sin in and of itself. We read in John 2:15 that even Jesus experienced anger when he made a whip and turned over the tables of the money changers. He drove them all out of His father's house, the temple.

It is the physical response of unbridled anger that is a sin. The difference is that anger, if not controlled, can turn into rage, a state where anger takes control of you, where the trouble lies.

Having adult children in your home can give cause for anger from time to time, especially when they are acting rebellious and immature. To feel anger is a natural emotion we all feel when someone's behavior or words are contrary to peace and truth. Adult children, as well as partners or officemates, can say or do things that trigger you. An angry response can cause emotional pain, but if not controlled, it can cause physical harm. I know people who are in prison because they let anger get out of control, and it ended in the death of another.

Rage is the emotional response that comes when anger is allowed to run free in our minds, which causes us to react violently to others. This is not only a sin, but it opens the door in our lives to the demonic spirits to come in and control us. It is called a fit of rage. Ephesians 4:27 goes on to tell us why we are not to let our anger control us. It says that if we do, it gives the devil a foothold in our lives. Other translations use the word opportunity. Rage is a sin that God will forgive, but if our actions harm or even kill another, we will not only find ourselves in prison but we'll also have to live with the memory of what we did to another, which will be especially painful if that person was a loved one.

When tempers flare, and anger shows up, you have a choice in that moment to remove yourself from the confrontation until you can get a grip on your emotions and cool down. We cannot, however, make others do the same. It takes a great measure of self-control in heated moments to calm ourselves or remove ourselves from the fight, but it is possible with the help of the Holy Spirit.

REFLECTIONS

+ We have all said things in anger that we don't really mean. We have probably surprised ourselves in what we've said or done in anger just as much as we've surprised, or hurt, the other person. Have you asked them to forgive you for your temper?

+ If you have a hard time controlling your temper, how can you seek out help to get it under control?

ACTION OF THE WEEK

Read Ephesians 4:17–32. It gives us some very specific ways to handle ourselves properly, such as speaking truthfully to our neighbor and not letting unwholesome talk come out of our mouths. Write down what the Lord shows you about yourself. What is He asking you to look deeper into or consider more carefully about yourself and your actions? Are there amends you need to start making?

GUIDED PRAYER

Dear God, I need the fruit of the Holy Spirit in my life to help me treat others the way I want to be treated. I want You to help me and empower me when I find myself in heated confrontations. Stay by my side and help me control my anger. Amen.

The Adoption Stigma

*For he chose us in him before the creation of the
world to be holy and blameless in his sight. In love he
predestined us for adoption to sonship through Jesus
Christ, in accordance with his pleasure and will . . .*

— *Ephesians 1:4–5*

COMMENTARY

As a child of the 1970s, I remember there was a stigma attached to
kids who were adopted. They were picked on and made to feel less
than others. I grew up with both of my birth parents, but I had a
friend in high school who was adopted at birth. He was the only son
and youngest child with three older sisters who were all born into
the family. As he grew up, his sisters despised him because he was
"Daddy's favorite" and a "spoiled brat." As he got older, I believe
he struggled with his identity because he really wanted to find his
birth parents to know where he came from.

No matter how "blended" a parent might work to make an
adopted child feel, sometimes, when the adopted child gets older,
they might begin to struggle with depression resulting from feelings of abandonment, or they may develop behavioral issues related
to their identity crisis. It is not uncommon for adopted children,
especially from foster care, to pull away from and shut out their
adopted parents as they become adults.

Adopted adult children need to hear this week's Bible verse
explained to them in the sense that just as God has chosen us, and
"adopted" us into His heavenly family, their parents have chosen
them to be a permanent member of their family. Birth parents don't
get to choose their children, but they do have the option to choose

who they adopt. Adopted children of all ages need to hear that they are loved just as much as if they were a biological child, and that they are wanted—even needed.

It is normal for adoptive parents to struggle with feelings of rejection by their adult child. As difficult as these emotions may be, parents need to try to see the situation from their child's perspective. It requires patience and understanding when their adopted children begin to ask questions about their birth parents, especially when they express a desire to reconnect with them. It is by no means a reflection of the care or situation surrounding the adoptive parent(s); rather, it's a need to understand the child's unknown past and connect their own dots. It is a good idea for parents to reach out for help as they try to help their adult child cope. A good counselor with experience in these matters will greatly help the parents take the appropriate steps to process their thoughts and emotions.

REFLECTIONS

✛ If you are the parent of an adopted adult child, have you already experienced these subjects and feelings? What other kinds of frustrations feel unique to adoptive families?

✛ If your adopted child sought out their birth parents, how have you helped them navigate their emotions during this time in their life? How have you navigated your own feelings?

ACTION OF THE WEEK

Read Ephesians 1:4–5 to your adopted child, no matter their age, and explain to them that just as God has chosen them to be His child, so you have chosen them above all others to be your child for life.

GUIDED PRAYER

Thank You, Father God, for choosing to adopt me and my children to be permanent members of Your family! Help my child understand the depths of Your love, as well as our love for them as their parents.

Speaking the Truth in Love

*Speaking the truth in love, we will grow to become
in every respect the mature body of him who is
the head, that is, Christ.*

— *Ephesians 4:15*

COMMENTARY

As Christian parents, we are admonished throughout scripture to raise our children in the path of righteousness and teach them the way of truth. As Proverbs 22:6 says, "and even when they are old they will not turn from it."

There comes a time as our children grow into adulthood that they might begin to question the teachings of the Bible, and even God. This is not always a bad thing, as it is indicative of their maturing process. Our children, just like us, want to discover that what they believe in is true, not just what they were told to believe. University professors often lead students to question everything, including their faith. It is in this transitional period that we must pray for our children's spiritual protection and make every effort to speak the truth to them in love. The Bible describes the Devil as the father of lies and says that many false teachers and deceivers have gone out into the world.

As our children are transitioning into adults, they are seeking identity and acceptance. The truth is, they are children of God, created in his image and likeness, given free will. They are fearfully and wonderfully made by the Creator of all life. Jesus is our Lord, our redeemer, the source of hope and new life. The enemy tries to distort the truth and tell our children that they are what they feel they are. The world teaches that there is no absolute truth and that truth is relative. As adults, we live according to our beliefs, so it is of extreme importance that we know and live according to the truth. Jesus said, "I am the way, the truth and the life. No one comes to the Father except through me."

As our adult children navigate their own path, we need to continue to speak the truth to them in love, while remembering that they are now responsible for their own decisions. Don't reject them if they become misguided or are living a lifestyle that is contrary to sound Biblical teaching. Trust they will eventually see past worldly temptations. Pray continually for God to reveal truth to them, and to protect them from all deception that would seek to destroy their faith. Never lose hope; Jesus is the mighty deliverer!

REFLECTIONS

✛ Have you taught your children in the truth of the scriptures? Are they walking in truth now, or are they choosing a different path?

✛ None of us are perfect parents, but praying fervently over our children is a powerful force attended to by God Himself.

ACTION OF THE WEEK

Devote time and effort to pray over each of your children's minds and hearts to be protected as they transition into adults, for God to expose falsehood, and for Him to reveal His truth to them.

GUIDED PRAYER

Father God, I place my children in Your hands. I trust You with their lives, to keep them in Your love and truth all the days of their lives. I thank You for never leaving their side. Amen.

The Discipline of the Lord

*Know then in your heart that as a man disciplines
his son, so the LORD your God disciplines you.*
— *Deuteronomy 8:5*

COMMENTARY

After my divorce at the age of 22, I was mad at God, and I walked away from Him for five years. I was making bad decisions that could easily have ended my life. I felt betrayed by love and allowed bitterness and depression to take its place. As I look back on my early life, I can remember His gentle rebukes, but I hardened my heart toward Him and rejected his discipline. He continued his pursuit of me, however, and I chose to relent and repent, allowing His love and correction to change me for good.

I continue to realize that, like you as a parent of adult children, I am still being parented by our heavenly Father. Discipline is not something we must only endure during childhood. We are to submit to the Lord's discipline throughout our lives. I believe that our proclivity to wander from the path is ever present, even as adults. For this reason, we need to lead by example, showing our adult children that we continually need His correction, guidance, and discipline in our own lives. This is a vital part of our relationship with God. He warns us several times in scripture not to harden our hearts, and He tells us that discipline is for our own good. For instance, Hebrews 12:11 acknowledges that while discipline might not exactly be pleasant, it's necessary, as, "Later on, however, it produces a harvest of righteousness and peace for those who have been trained by it." A hardened heart leads to rebellion and straying from the life God wants for us.

We should be open and honest with our adult children and tell them of the ways we resisted the discipline of the Lord. We need to share how He saved us and changed us when we accepted it. Hebrews 12:8 says that if we reject the discipline of the Lord, then we are not His true sons and daughters. Let your kids know that if they want to live each day in the love and grace of God, they should be willing to endure his correction until it becomes a matter of self-discipline. This is the sign of maturity as a true son or daughter. One of the great things about His discipline is that he always does it out of love.

Your grown children need to learn that discipline is a lifelong lesson that will develop their character and keep them on the right path for their own good, while helping them model the path for their children, too.

REFLECTIONS

+ How has the Lord disciplined you in the past? Were you receptive to it?

+ Sharing your story of God disciplining you with your adult children will be a model for their own lives to follow. When did you last stray from God, and how were you disciplined to return to faith?

ACTION OF THE WEEK

Think back, then write down your own stories of God's discipline in your life, and share them with your adult children. Show them how your life was made better by receiving the discipline of the Lord. Show them how your imperfections still keep you loved!

GUIDED PRAYER

Father, I take comfort in knowing I am Your child because of Your discipline in my life. Help me be receptive and obedient when I need it, and help me model it for my own children. Amen.

Nonverbal Communication

A happy heart makes the face cheerful,
but heartache crushes the spirit.
— *Proverbs 15:13*

COMMENTARY

We all deal with a vast array of emotions every day. We might start our day with joyful optimism and then stub our toe getting out of bed! How quickly our circumstances affect our emotions. Some people share their emotions by speaking their mind, without regarding the feelings of others. Some worry too much about what others might think, so they never say what they really feel.

This is why police detectives receive training on how to read body language. A person's nonverbal cues can tell investigators when a person is lying or hiding something. Our nonverbal communication speaks louder than our words. As parents, we've learned to read our children's nonverbal cues. They might be saying the right things, but their body language will tell us they aren't being honest. For instance, a high-school friend and I were questioned by police about spray paint on a wall. I denied it but noticed I had paint on my fingers, so I stuffed them into my pockets.

When it comes to conflict and negative feelings in the parent–adult child relationship, we need to realize that our body language always tells the truth. I am one of the many people who are not gifted with a "poker face." My body language often tells my wife when I'm irritated or not really listening to her. People like me can either practice our poker face, or we can learn to control our emotional responses. In the life of a believer, this is called self-control and is a fruit of the Holy Spirit. I admit I have also been guilty of giving others the silent treatment. My mother would say, "If you don't have anything nice to say, say nothing at all." But while maintaining silence might avoid a big fight, it does not take away the negative emotions that are expressed through closed-off body language.

When in disagreement with your adult child's behavior, try to be conscientious of your body language. You don't want them to feel rejected or sense you aren't being truthful by your folded arms and the scowl on your face while telling them their pile of dirty laundry doesn't bother you. There is a time and place to have difficult conversations, but if your body language does not match your words, maybe waiting is the best choice. We cannot expect our children to exhibit honest self-control if we don't practice it ourselves.

REFLECTIONS

* Learning and practicing self-control when it comes to difficult conversations takes time and practice to develop. It might mean turning around and coming back in a few minutes after you've cooled off, when you're ready to have a calmer conversation.

* How good are you at nonverbal communication? Does your body language match the words you say? What areas need improvement?

ACTION OF THE WEEK

Make an effort to practice positive body language with different people this week. Perhaps you can spend some time in the mirror seeing your face as you think about strong emotions. Also, practice reading the nonverbal cues of others around you. Do you find anything surprising?

GUIDED PRAYER

Lord, You know me better than anyone. Please help me produce the fruit of honest self-control as I interact with my family. Amen.

Dysfunctional Families: Codependent Adult Children

*Jacob said to his father, "I am Esau your firstborn.
I have done as you told me. Please sit up and eat some
of my game, so that you may give me your blessing."*
— *Genesis 27:19*

COMMENTARY

Genesis 27 depicts several instances of dysfunction and code-pendency in the family of Isaac, his wife Rebekah, and their two adult sons, Esau and Jacob. Isaac was nearing the end of his life and had become blind. Rebekah was a rather controlling mother, still telling her adult son Jacob what to do. Jacob's codependency became apparent in that he was complicit in his mother's deceitful plot to obtain his father's (important, inheritance-based) blessing. It was traditional for the father to pronounce a special blessing on his firstborn son. Esau, Isaac's firstborn, was very hairy while Jacob was not. Rebekah put lamb's wool on Jacob in order to trick her blind husband into blessing her younger, favorite son, Jacob. Because of their successful scheme, Esau missed out on his bless-ing, became enraged with his brother, and plotted to kill him.

Jacob was so codependent on his controlling mother that he lied to his father and pretended to be his brother.

While this story depicts some of the extreme forms of dys-function and codependency, we often see similar traits in our own families. When adult children depend on their parents to meet their physical and emotional needs, they feed the cycle of dysfunction. They may use guilt and blame the parents for their own inabilities and insecurities. They manipulate their parents into feeding the cycle by always playing the victim. As long as this is allowed to continue, the adult child will never take responsibility for themselves.

At its root, codependency is the byproduct of placing dependence on another person, instead of God, to meet one's needs. God wants us to find our self-worth in how He sees us. He also wants us to rely on His provision and guidance for our lives. When we live in alignment with His Word, and prioritize our relationships accordingly, He will provide all our needs, for both parent and child, in a peaceful and healthy way that brings Him glory.

REFLECTIONS

✝ In what ways do your family relationships bear the scars of codependency and dysfunction? Odds are codependents don't realize how much they rely on others and might even deny that there's a problem. Dysfunction is a little easier to notice because, by definition, it means something isn't working right, even if it's been working that way for a long time. It's not your place to point out other people's relationship issues, but sometimes it's easier to first see the signs of dysfunction in others before we can see or address it in our own family.

✝ Do you depend on God to meet your physical and emotional needs, or have you relied on your parents or children to meet them instead?

ACTION OF THE WEEK

Ask God to show you any unhealthy, misplaced expectations in your relationships and write them down. Then ask for His wisdom in how to make the necessary changes, starting today.

GUIDED PRAYER

Father God, I want Your help in my family so that we can have healthy, well-balanced relationships. Show me what needs to change and help me see those changes through. Amen.

Dysfunctional Families: Codependent Parents

"Prepare me the kind of tasty food I like and bring it to me to eat, so that I may give you my blessing before I die."

— *Genesis 27:4*

COMMENTARY

Continuing the discussion of the dysfunctional relationships in Isaac's family, we learn that Isaac was blind and depended on his son Esau to hunt and provide food. Isaac knew that he was nearing his death, and that his eldest son Esau expected his father to bless him. However, Isaac withheld his blessing until his son met his needs by first hunting game and then preparing his favorite meal. Even though his blessing was expected, Isaac made it a reward-based blessing.

While it is common for adult children to help their elderly parents with their physical needs, sometimes the parent will use guilt or shame to manipulate their children to get what they want. It is also common for parents to place an unhealthy reliance on their children to meet their emotional needs, instead of relying on God. It is because of the natural love a child has for their parent that the adult child overlooks their parents' manipulation. This can cause resentment and frustration for the adult child and can be the cause of conflict in the relationship. For instance, not all elderly parents are too feeble to care for themselves but might suffer from their own life choices, such as addictions, and the adult child might feel obligated to step in and help, even if it puts the child at a disadvantage. Not all parents are mentally healthy, causing the children to take on the burden of caring for their parents and siblings at an early age. This hampers the emotional growth of the child, who may later fall into the same addictive lifestyle as their parents and/or manipulate their own children to fulfill their unmet emotional needs.

Rebekah's age is not evident from the story, but we can see that she used manipulation and control over her grown son Jacob. In verse 13 she told Jacob to obey her even though he knew it was wrong and feared the outcome. She said, "My son, let the curse fall on me. Just do what I say; go and get them for me."

Like malignant cancers, dysfunction and codependency cannot be prevented from showing up in our families, but awareness, early detection, and refusing to feed them are the best ways to keep them from growing.

REFLECTIONS

+ Was your family affected by dysfunction or codependency during your childhood? How far back, generationally, do you think it started?

+ Are you willing to be the one to break the cycle in your family?

ACTION OF THE WEEK

Spend some time evaluating yourself, and then your family members, for areas affected by this subject. If you aren't sure, ask God to show you. Write down any insights, and make a plan to start one change this week.

GUIDED PRAYER

Father, I ask You to open my eyes to see my family relationships as they truly are. I ask You to work through me to break the cycle of codependency and dysfunction. Amen.

Suddenly!

Suddenly there was such a violent earthquake that the foundations of the prison were shaken. At once all the prison doors flew open, and everyone's chains came loose.

— *Acts 16:26*

COMMENTARY

Chapter 16 of the book of Acts tells the story of how Paul and Silas were arrested, beaten, and thrown into prison for preaching about Jesus and causing "civil unrest." They very easily could have gotten angry or depressed, blaming God for allowing this to happen to them, but instead they chose to worship Him in song and pray to Him around midnight. Their actions caused a shift in the atmosphere. The act of their worship caused God to move suddenly! He sent a major earthquake that set the captives free. In the end, the jailer in charge of guarding them became a believer, and he and his whole household were saved that day.

Maybe you have a son or daughter in prison, or maybe they are bound by the shackles of addiction, depression, or torment. I want to encourage you to never give up and never lose hope. If anyone had a reason to lose hope it was Paul and Silas. Like them, make a choice to worship God in the face of what seems a hopeless situation, because God is still all-powerful. Maybe your children are not walking with God; perhaps they are unbelievers and are living their lives and raising their families without God. Never stop praying and believing for them. God never sleeps. He hears your prayers and receives your worship as you patiently await a "suddenly" moment for your children.

Whether your adult children live with you or not, you can begin to change the atmosphere in your home and family by playing worship music and singing and praying aloud. It shouldn't be in an "in your face" way, but rather to model "this is what brings me joy." When you turn on the light, darkness flees, filling your home with brightness as you invite His presence in. The Bible says God inhabits the praises of His people, so praise Him in every circumstance, and give thanks for all He has done in your life, and for all He will do in the lives of your adult children!

We have Hannah, the mother of the Prophet Samuel as an example of the success of zealous prayer. She wept bitterly and prayed fervently for a son, and when the Lord answered her prayer, she dedicated her son to God for all the days of his life. It's never too late to commit your children to God and pray for their "suddenly" moment.

REFLECTIONS

✦ If God can raise the dead, He definitely can break the chains that bind us and open our prison doors. What is tying you or your children down?

✦ Prayer and worship are powerful spiritual weapons. Use them to change the atmosphere inside your heart and mind.

ACTION OF THE WEEK

Read the story in Acts 16:16–40. Now, try something completely different: spend some time in prayer and worship, not asking for anything but just loving God for who He is.

GUIDED PRAYER

Lord, I feel Your presence, and I thank You for everything You have already done, and will do, for me. Amen.

The Banquet Table

You prepare a table before me in the presence
of my enemies. You anoint my head with oil;
my cup overflows.

— *Psalm 23:5*

COMMENTARY

Imagine William Wallace (played by Mel Gibson in *Braveheart*) giving his freedom speech while facing off against King Edward the First, and then sitting down to enjoy a full-course feast with his soldiers right there on the battlefield. That is literally what this verse is telling us. As believers and parents, we also face a vast army of enemies, but they don't face us on a battlefield. Instead, they lay traps and ambush us from the shadows. And our enemies aren't exactly people, either, but ill will and pain personified.

Whether you are struggling with a stubborn adult child who is a major contributor to anxiety and stress in your life, or you are battling depression and loneliness because the loss of your children due to death or their own choice to stay away, the concept is the same. Today your enemies might be high anxiety or deep depression, and tomorrow they may be fear and hopelessness. Whatever name your enemy has, God has the opposite set out on His banquet table for your nourishment. When fear hits you, have a double helping of peace. If depression or grief are choking you, take a drink from the cup of the joy of the Lord. If worry or emptiness attack, feast on His promise to supply all your needs according to His riches in Christ Jesus.

Jesus modeled this concept for us the night before His crucifixion, when He shared the Passover Feast with His disciples, even in the presence of Judas, who would betray Him with a kiss. Jesus used two elements of that feast to commemorate forever the New Covenant, with the bread and wine representing His body and blood. It is commonly called the Lord's Table, or the Lord's Supper, in the church. In the sacrifice of His body, He brought healing and resurrection, providing victory over the enemies' sickness and death. His blood, bringing forgiveness and restoration, broke the power of sin.

There is a glorious banquet that awaits all of Jesus' followers in Heaven, when we will be reunited with our King Jesus and all loved ones who have gone before us. It is the Great Feast, the Marriage Supper of the Lamb, when all our pain and "enemies" will have been utterly and eternally defeated.

REFLECTIONS

✛ Consider again the concept that an enemy might not be a person but how that person makes us feel. What are some of the names of the enemies that have attacked you?

✛ What delicacy on God's table do you want to taste today?

ACTION OF THE WEEK

Write down what poison the enemy has been trying to feed you, and then write down what you want the Lord to pass down the table to you. Ask for it in prayer.

GUIDED PRAYER

Father God, I am blessed to know that You are so not worried about my enemies that You would create a feast for me to enjoy even when they have surrounded me. I am truly thankful for Your protection and all Your great provisions for me. Amen.

Honoring Your Child

He received honor and glory from God the Father when the voice came to him from the Majestic Glory, saying, "This is my Son, whom I love; with him I am well pleased."

— *2 Peter 1:17*

COMMENTARY

Jesus knew His purpose on earth, and He embraced His call with perfect obedience to God the Father. It had to be comforting and reassuring to hear His Father's voice blessing and honoring Him, telling Him that He loves Him and is proud of Him.

As you have read several entries in this book, you might be thinking how glad you are that you have not had to deal with many of these issues with your own child or children. I don't believe that having mature, well-adjusted children is due to chance or luck. It is often a reflection of good parenting. It should be viewed as a reward for all the hard work you put in to be a good parent. But good parenting never guarantees a perfect child.

If you have raised well-adjusted children, they made the job of parenting so much easier. It is good to praise and honor our Heavenly Father for the joy our adult children have brought us, but don't forget to honor and praise your children! They need to hear your words of affirmation even as adults. If they are still practicing and implementing godly principles in their life choices, they should be commended and applauded by the parents. If your child didn't turn out as you'd hoped, they still need to hear words of affirmation. God simply isn't done with them yet! You can still find the good qualities you admire in them and commend and applaud them.

I am very happy with my three adult children, and how they have turned out. They each have made me very proud to be their dad, many times over. I love seeing their faces light up when I tell them how proud I am of them and praise their godly character. It must feel good to them and empower them to keep staying the course.

Words of affirmation is one of the five love languages, and it is my biggest one, but it doesn't have to be your adult child's love language for you to tell them how much they bring you joy and how proud you are of their accomplishments. Everyone is their own worst critic. Your children are no different; they need to hear you bless them and honor them. Like a ray of sunshine on a cloudy day, it will brighten their countenance and help them see the good in their own life. Even if your adult child is not walking the straight and narrow way right now, find something praiseworthy in their life that made you feel proud.

REFLECTIONS

✦ When was the last time you remember praising and honoring your adult child? Do you remember their reaction when you did? It probably made you feel just as good!

✦ What godly characteristics do they have? Write them down.

ACTION OF THE WEEK

Find a time this week to praise your adult child in the presence of others. Mention their good characteristics and qualities that you've written down.

GUIDED PRAYER

Father God, help me see my children as You see them. Bring to my mind the attributes or accomplishments that make me proud of them, and remind me to praise them. Amen.

The Fear of Man

Fear of man will prove to be a snare,
but whoever trusts in the LORD is kept safe.
— *Proverbs 29:25*

COMMENTARY

Many adult children struggle with being vulnerable with their parents because they fear judgment or criticism. These fears are usually founded in past negative experiences. The parent may have criticized their ideas, saying things like "That's the dumbest thing I've ever heard," or "Surely you can't be serious." Instances like these tend to stick in the mind of the hurt or offended child, causing them to guard their true thoughts and feelings. These hurtful words cause feelings of rejection and invalidity that can stay present into adulthood. It makes them not want to share their true thoughts and emotions with their parents, or anyone else for that matter. Repeated instances like these will cause them to say what they think the parent wants to hear, instead of the truth. They are then living a lie, trapped in a performance mentality and a fear of what others think of them. The result is shallow, manufactured relationships instead of genuine ones in which they feel free to express their inner thoughts and truest feelings.

If you have damaged your relationship with your adult child due to similar criticisms, you might still be able to reverse the trajectory of the relationship if you take the appropriate steps. You must first acknowledge and take responsibility for your words and actions toward them. An apology can go a long way, but it is only the beginning of the renewal process. Secondly, you need to reaffirm them by telling them that their true feelings are what you seek. Tell them that you love them for who they are, not for who they perceive you want them to be. Lastly, you can validate their emotions and feelings by letting them express them without any judgment. Their thoughts may not line up with yours, but they are who they are, and their thoughts are just as valid as yours are to you.

It is never too late to say I'm sorry and try again. Admitting your shortcomings as a parent and asking for their forgiveness is teaching them the proper way to come to God for themselves.

Repairing a strained relationship with adult children who are truly trapped in a negative self-image will take some time. Only after they see you truly want to know them and accept them for who they really are, will they gradually feel comfortable opening up to you. Setting them free from the fear of others starts with you.

REFLECTIONS

+ Does your adult child hide their true feelings from you and shut you out? How can you tell?

+ Are you willing to begin the process of restoring your relationship? They can't initiate or respond openly to you until they are first set free from their fear of others.

ACTION OF THE WEEK

Plan a time to sit down with a child that is closed off, and apologize for things you have said or done that caused them to feel unaccepted for who they are. Don't talk about who was "right" or "wrong," other than admitting it was wrong for you to say or do those things. Allow them to take the conversation from there.

GUIDED PRAYER

Father, help me see my part in causing my child to hide their true feelings from me. Help them be able to open up to me and begin again to share who they are on the inside. Help me accept and love them as they are. Amen.

Amazing Grace

> *But by the grace of God I am what I am,*
> *and his grace to me was not without effect.*
> *No, I worked harder than all of them—yet not I,*
> *but the grace of God that was with me.*
> — *1 Corinthians 15:10*

COMMENTARY

As believers, we are all given a measure of the grace of God. Ephesians 4:7 says, "But to each one of us grace has been given as Christ apportioned it." You may have heard sermons about grace being the unmerited favor of God. It is also the empowering force in us that enables us and equips us for acts of obedience to Him. In other words, grace empowers. It empowers us to repent of sin and live in the righteousness that He provides. It also empowers us to do hard things like turning the other cheek and forgiving others.

Have you been a good steward of the grace given to you as a parent? Grace is given to us as parents to be coworkers with God in building character in the lives of our children.

Therefore, we have a responsibility to build them up with words of affirmation and power. Grace-filled words should instill self-confidence in our children, teaching them that by God's grace to them, they can do whatever God has for them with boldness, knowing that He has their back and will empower them in whatever circumstance they find themselves. Grace lifts up and strengthens them to face life's struggles, like peer pressure or sexual temptations. Living in God's grace requires self-denial in the sense of not trusting in our own abilities. Our own efforts will always fall short of what God intends for us. In fact, grace is how we are saved, through proclaiming our faith in what Christ did for us, not trusting in our own works to make us good enough (Ephesians 2:8–9).

When interacting with your adult child, you can rely on the empowering grace God has given you to overlook their shortcomings and, instead, point out all the attributes and character that you see God has gifted them with. As they transition into their own autonomy, you can encourage them that with God they can do anything, even the impossible. If they grasp this truth, they will realize that His grace is sufficient for them in everything.

REFLECTIONS

✛ Grace is the literal power of God working in and through us, equipping us and empowering us to live for Him.

✛ How have you extended this grace to your adult child? Have you empowered them with confidence in God to face life's challenges?

ACTION OF THE WEEK

Read the following verses and write down what you learn from them, then share it with your adult child: Ephesians 2:8–9, 1 Corinthians 3:9–15, and Romans 12:6–8.

GUIDED PRAYER

Thank You, God, for Your amazing grace in my life. Help me be a good steward of that grace, and help me pour Your grace on

_____.

Releasing Unrealistic Expectations

Then some of the believers who belonged to the party of the Pharisees stood up and said, "The Gentiles must be circumcised and required to keep the law of Moses."

— *Acts 15:5*

COMMENTARY

This verse describes a debate held at the Council at Jerusalem in regard to new Gentile believers coming to faith in Christ. A Gentile is anyone not born a Jew. The debate was over whether these Gentiles had to adhere to the commandments in the Law of Moses, given to the Jews. In verse 10, Peter stood up and said, "Now then, why do you try to test God by putting on the necks of Gentiles a yoke that neither we nor our ancestors have been able to bear?" The context of this passage is saying to not put expectations on others that God does not expect of them.

We all have fallen victim to unrealistic expectations placed on us by others, or even ourselves. When we are too rigid in our expectations, we set ourselves and others up to fail. No one can be perfect in their performance, always, no matter what it may be. When we fail to measure up to those expectations, we feel like a failure, causing us to want to quit trying to meet them. Did God give the Law of Moses to show that no one can meet high expectations all the time? The New Testament shows it was to demonstrate our inability to meet them. Through perfect obedience to the Law, Jesus was able to fulfill the Law for us and offer us new life through faith in Him.

We can place unrealistic expectations on our adult children when we expect that by a certain age they should have a college degree, a career, and a family of their own—especially when we did not teach and prepare them to do so. Maybe they don't share your goals for their lives. After all, the life you are living now may or may not measure up to the expectations of your parents.

There are realistic expectations you are right to require of your adult child, such as getting a job, paying rent, saving money, and taking responsibility for their own share of expenses, like gas and car insurance. But who they will become, and when, is up to them. Remember to encourage and show some grace and leniency when they fail, and inspire them to get back up and try again.

REFLECTIONS

✤ When faced with unrealistic expectations, we set ourselves up for failure. How have you failed to meet your own expectations, or those of your parents? What would have made those goals more realistic?

✤ You can help your adult child succeed by helping them set realistic goals for themselves, and by allowing room for failures.

ACTION OF THE WEEK

Write down the ways you have failed to meet unrealistic expectations in the past. Then forgive yourself for those inevitable failures. Have you placed similar unattainable goals on your child? Rethink and adjust the expectations you place on your adult children as needed, and let them know your new perspective.

GUIDED PRAYER

Thank You, Jesus, for covering all my failures to measure up to God's standards. Help me set realistic expectations on _____ and forgive their failures to measure up to the impossible task.

Giving and Receiving Love

We love because he first loved us.

— *1 John 4:19*

COMMENTARY

Many adult children as well as parents have difficulty either giving or receiving love. What might be easy to do as a child gets harder to do as adults, because we are hampered either by our own sins or the sins and hurts of others. Our ability to give or receive love gets tainted and damaged over time, and if not healed and repaired, we can grow emotionally numb. When we sin against or hurt those we love, we tend to struggle with regret and unworthiness. When we sin against God, we can feel unworthy of His love. It is also the same in our earthly relationships.

In the story of the prodigal son in Luke 15, we see this truth played out in the mindset of the son. In verse 21 he said, "Father, I have sinned against heaven and against you. I am no longer worthy to be called your son." We can experience the same feelings of guilt over our own sins and are too ashamed of ourselves to come to God and receive His love and forgiveness. It is our own brokenness that keeps us from receiving the full benefits of His love for us.

If your adult son or daughter struggles with giving or receiving love, you can help them get to a healthy place of giving and receiving. It requires them seeing and receiving the truth of the love of God in His Word. If we don't learn to receive the unconditional love of God first, we will settle for natural human love, which is often conditional.

Another way to help your adult child express and receive love is to speak their "love language." This term was coined by Dr. Gary Chapman in his books on the five love languages, which are physical touch, words of affirmation, quality time, gift giving, and acts of service. Since we all respond to one or more of these, it is beneficial to discover the love language of our adult child and speak their language instead of speaking our own love language to them and then wondering why they don't respond the way we would.

REFLECTIONS

✢ Do you or your adult child have difficulty when it comes to expressing and receiving love? Have you ever discussed unconditional love with them? Have you expressed and offered true, unconditional love?

✢ Helping them receive the love of God is paramount to the healthy exercise of giving and receiving unconditional love.

ACTION OF THE WEEK

Research "love languages." What is yours? Did you know before you looked it up? Write down your adult children's love languages. Since we all have our own "love language," it may take some time to understand that no matter how great you are at sharing your love, your language might not be the way the other person understands, expresses, and feels love. The same is true for how you understand and interpret the way others express their love to you. Maybe you've just been miscommunicating! It will take effort to learn how to best apply or translate your language to theirs. Once you've reviewed the five types, demonstrate three ways you can speak (each of) your children's love language this week.

GUIDED PRAYER

Thank You, Father, for giving me and my family your unconditional, perfect love. Help me and my child(ren) learn to give and receive Your kind of love to others. Amen.

Defeating Digital Demons

*But if you harbor bitter envy and selfish ambition in
your hearts, do not boast about it or deny the truth.
Such "wisdom" does not come down from heaven
but is earthly, unspiritual, demonic.*

— *James 3:14–15*

COMMENTARY

While the Bible does not address the modern advancements of the
digital age, it does address many of the underlying symptoms of
them on our hearts, minds, and relationships. This verse addresses
two such symptoms, envy and selfishness, and calls them earthly,
unspiritual, and demonic.

The Internet, social media, and online gaming are not demonic in
and of themselves; however, they can be and often are tools used by
the enemy to cause mental and emotional harm to us. For instance, if a
partner spends too much time on social media platforms like Facebook
and Instagram, they can find themselves getting jealous or envious
of how other people's lives appear, while forgetting that most people
only post pics of the good things they experience. They don't often post
about their own struggles and failures. An adult child living with mom
and dad can spend hours gaming online with their friends instead of
looking for work or helping out with household chores, while dad is in
his man cave or office "dealing with work" as he views pornography on
the Internet. These are just a few examples of the digital demons I'm
referring to. They all have the additional harm of alienating the family
members left alone while the user spends all that time online.

Too much social media can cause emotional insecurity, jealousy,
and loneliness. Too much time spent on online gaming wastes days

of time, and hundreds if not thousands of dollars eventually, and causes frustration and resentment. The dad addicted to porn is likewise robbed of the real intimacy and satisfaction God intended for his marriage. All these technologies can be beneficial, but if not managed well and tightly controlled, they will devour the quality time and social interactions of the family. The consequence could be a wife or husband allured into an extramarital affair, whether emotional or sexual in nature, ending in a divorce. Too much gaming can lead to gaming addiction—yes, that is a real thing—and an unrealistic worldview, stunting the emotional and mental growth needed to help the adult child prepare for the real world that awaits them.

These digital demons all culminate in the isolation of the individual from the family. "If a house is divided against itself, that house cannot stand" (Mark 3:25).

REFLECTIONS

☀ Has digital technology robbed you or your family in any of the ways mentioned? How much time each day would you say is negatively affected by technology?

☀ Which digital demons need to be cast out of your lives?

ACTION OF THE WEEK

Keep track of online time for everyone in the family this week. Add it up to get one family number (not per person). Have a serious discussion with your adult child and family about how much time, attention, and money is being "sacrificed" to these digital demons. Then make a plan to set boundaries and reclaim your relationship with digital tools.

GUIDED PRAYER

Father God, forgive me for the time I've wasted on meaningless and harmful things. Help me and my adult child face the reality of these dangers, and help us put them in their place outside of our relationship.

Perseverance in Parenting

Therefore, since we are surrounded by such a great
cloud of witnesses, let us throw off everything that
hinders and the sin that so easily entangles. And let us
run with perseverance the race marked out for us . . .
— Hebrews 12:1

COMMENTARY

This week's verse speaks of the need for perseverance in the context of running a race. Just as a long-distance runner needs perseverance to press through the pain and find that "second breath" to keep going to the finish line, parenting can seem much like a race. We want our family to move forward and succeed. We inspire our children to do their best at school and learn the lessons that will prepare them for adulthood. We can feel like we are nearing the finish line when they graduate from high school and move off to college or a job. But maybe things don't work out like we anticipate. Sometimes our adult children aren't developmentally ready to strike out on their own. They may have struggles and setbacks that hinder their progress. The necessity to provide and assist our adult children might wear our patience thin from financial or emotional stress. During times like this, parents need to press into their relationship with God to find the necessary strength and steadfastness to carry them through. Isaiah 40:31 says, "but those who hope in the LORD will renew their strength. They will soar on wings like eagles; they will run and not grow weary, they will walk and not be faint."

There is also the "great cloud of witnesses" mentioned in Hebrews 12:1. These are the family members and support groups in the church who can encourage you as a parent to keep pressing on to the goal. Many churches offer free counseling or support groups for parents and adult children, but we have to be humble during these situations and ask for help. There are many parents who have been in your shoes and can offer sound advice to help you and your adult children succeed. These people are like those on the sidelines of a marathon, who run alongside you with a drink of water and encourage you to keep going. A parent's job is never really done, as we have a legacy in our potential grandchildren and should be there to support our adult children as they begin their own families, offering wisdom and perhaps even financial support when needed.

REFLECTIONS

+ It is easy to want to quit running our race when we get discouraged or face setbacks as parents. Who is part of the "cloud of witnesses" that can help you when you feel like quitting?

+ Parenting is not always easy, but when you catch your second wind and set your mind on finishing the race, you can find the strength and support to carry on and finish well.

ACTION OF THE WEEK

It's been said it takes a village to raise a child. Write a thank-you card of appreciation for someone who has supported and encouraged you when you felt like giving up. Even an out-of-the-blue text will be appreciated!

GUIDED PRAYER

Thank You, Lord, for continuing to give me the strength I need, and thank You for giving me a great cloud of witnesses to help me run my race. Amen.

The Secret of Contentment

I know what it is to be in need, and I know what it is to have plenty. I have learned the secret of being content in any and every situation, whether well fed or hungry, whether living in plenty or in want.

— *Philippians 4:12*

COMMENTARY

When we give our lives to Christ, it doesn't mean that we are saved from life's struggles, heartaches, and pain, but He saves us through them all. It is in going through hard times that we learn what it means to be content in any situation life brings. As the parent of an adult child, you will have undoubtedly had many opportunities to feel overwhelmed, taken for granted, and maybe abused by them. We invest our time, our hearts, and our money into raising well-adjusted adult children.

The secret to learning contentment in everything is to learn to give it all to God. We may not have the wisdom to know how to help them, but He does, and He has promised to give it to you when you ask. We cannot heal their broken hearts, but He can if we lead them to Him. We cannot control the outcome of their lives, and it isn't our place to try. It is in the letting go and trusting God with our lives and the future of our grown children that we experience true contentment in Him. You can trust Him to carry you through and trust Him with the life of your adult child as well. Philippians 1:6 says, "Being confident of this, that he who began a good work in you will carry it on to completion until the day of Christ Jesus."

Ultimately, you must reach a point when you have done all you can to love, nurture, and raise your children to know and follow the

Lord. After that, you are not responsible for the outcome of their lives. They are. They have watched you model what it means to be an adult and a believer. They have seen your successes and your shortcomings, and if they implement what you have taught them, they will have a good foundation for their own success. You have to learn the art of "letting go and letting God."

There is a contentment for the parent who acknowledges that they have done their part and that God will do His part. It is looking back at your life, at all the times the Lord has provided for your needs and carried you through life's bumps and bruises, successes and failures, that you will see that God has raised you as His own adult child. Trust He is helping you raise yours.

REFLECTIONS

+ You are God's adult child, who He has loved, raised, and equipped as a parent. How does that make you feel?

+ Have you learned the secret to being content in all things? Learning to be content and then teaching this to your adult child will benefit you both greatly.

ACTION OF THE WEEK

Write down all the ways you can think of that God has shown Himself faithful and trustworthy to carry you through difficult times. Share some of them with your adult child to let them know how much they, too, are loved.

GUIDED PRAYER

Thank You, Father, for carrying me throughout my life, teaching me to be content in every situation, and for helping me as I raise my own adult child. Amen.

RESOURCES

There are many resources available to help you grow in your faith walk with God. There are various books, websites, and apps available on godly parenting specific to adult children. Here are just a few I recommend.

BOOKS

The Hebrew-Greek Key Word Study Bible
A series of guides for many Bible translations, useful in studying the scriptures in the context of the languages they were written in. Key words in each verse are coded to *Strong's Concordance*.

Prayers That Heal the Heart *by Mark and Patti Virkler*
A great book that was used as curriculum in my life coaching certification.

Prayers That Avail Much to Overcome Anxiety and Depression
by Germaine Copeland (Word Ministries Inc.)
A book that will help improve your prayer life.

Praying the Scriptures for Your Adult Children: Trusting God with the Ones You Love *by Jodie Berndt*
Another book that will help improve your prayer life.

U.S. Department of Health & Human Services (MentalHealth.gov)

The U.S. Mental Health website offers hotlines and help for many mental health needs, in several languages.

Anxiety and Depression Association (ADAA.org)

Anxiety and Depression Association of America offers statistics, treatment options, "triumphing through science, treatment, and education."

Blue Letter Bible (BlueLetterBible.org)

This website promotes the study of God's Word with powerful tools, including an online reference library. You can also download the app on your phone.

Ultimate Freedom Coaching (UFC-Life-Coach.com)

Ultimate Freedom Coaching offers live in-person or virtual Christian life coach advice and help.

REFERENCES

Anxiety & Depression Association of America. "Facts &
    Statistics." Accessed November 26, 2021. ADAA.org
    /understanding-anxiety/facts-statistics.

Colorblind Guide. "Colorblind People Population! Statistics."
    Accessed October 19, 2021. ColorblindGuide.com/post
    /colorblind-people-population-live-counter.

DeCarlo, Dawn K., Mark Swanson, Gerald McGwin, Kristina
    Visscher, and Cynthia Owsley. "ADHD and Vision Problems
    in the National Survey of Children's Health." *Optometry and
    Vision* Science 93, no. 5 (May 2016): 459–465. doi:10.1097
    /OPX.0000000000000823.

National Suicide Prevention Lifeline. "Talk to Someone Now."
    Accessed September 22, 2021. SuicidePreventionLifeline.org
    /talk-to-someone-now.

Searing, Linda. "The Big Number: Lefties Make Up about
    10 Percent of the World." *The Washington Post*. August 12, 2019.
    WashingtonPost.com/health/the-big-number-lefties-make-up
    -about-10-percent-of-the-world/2019/08/09/69978100-b9e2
    -11e9-bad6-609f75bfd97f_story.html.

Wang, Shirley S. "The Health Risks of Being Left-Handed."
    The Wall Street Journal. December 6, 2011. WSJ.com/articles
    /SB10001424052970204083204577080562692452538.

Acknowledgments

I would like to thank first and foremost my Lord and Savior Jesus Christ, the author of my faith and my life story. Next, I want to thank my parents for their love and support, sweat, and tears, and for helping shape the man I am today. Special thanks to my wife for sticking with me while God sorts me out: you are my cheerleader and sounding board, and I couldn't have done it without you. I also want to thank my children for the joy you bring to my life. You each make me proud to be your Dad. Thank you to all the mentors and brothers and sisters in Christ who have sharpened me, prayed for me, and stood by me through it all.

About the Author

JAMIE CLOYD has been happily married for 25 years to his lovely wife, Shanna. He is also the father of three adult children, two beautiful daughters and his son; all of them love the Lord and serve His people. Jamie is an ordained pastor/teacher and a Certified Christian Life Coach, and he has been the host of a weekly men's Bible study group for the past six years.